Early Childhood
Vocabulary
Development
Activities

Literacy, Language, & Learning

salty

sour

sweet

Author

Molly A. Mackay

SHELL EDUCATION

Publishing Credits

Dona Herweck Rice, *Editor-in-Chief*; Lee Aucoin, *Creative Director*; Don Tran, *Print Production Manager*; Timothy J. Bradley, *Illustration Manager*; Jodene Smith, M.A., *Editor*; Leslie Huber, M.A., *Assistant Editor*; Lee Aucoin, *Cover Designer*; Robin Erickson, *Interior Layout Designer*; Corinne Burton, M.S. Ed., *Publisher*

Standards Compendium, Copyright 2004 McREL

Shell Education
5301 Oceanus Drive
Huntington Beach, CA 92649-1030
http://www.shelleducation.com
ISBN 978-1-4258-0700-9
©2010 Shell Educational Publishing, Inc.

Table of Contents

Introduction and Research

It is important that students be actively engaged in the process of vocabulary acquisition and that a child's "encounters with words should be playful, so as to provoke a curiosity and an interest in word study" (Anderson & Nagy 1993). What better way to provoke this curiosity than with enjoyable games and activities carefully structured by the classroom teacher? The activities throughout this book were created with this idea in mind. **Each lesson includes a suggested vocabulary list related to a topic that is correlated to both national and state standards.**

Cross-curricular topics were selected to include **vocabulary in language arts, math, and science.** The lesson for each topic is designed to provide opportunities for students to play with the vocabulary words. Adaptations or extensions for each lesson are included at the end of each teacher direction page so that students may have chances for repeated exposure to the vocabulary words that were ntroduced. The section titled "Beyond the Book" includes three other ideas for fostering vocabulary development. Each idea can be used in conjunction with the lessons presented here. They can also be used independently of the lessons. These ideas represent strategies for students to develop *word consciousness*. Word consciousness as defined by Graves and Watts-Taffe (2002) means having an awareness about and an interest in words and their meanings. These authors suggest that students who develop this word consciousness are basically developing positive attitudes about words and can become more successful in "expanding the breadth and depth of their word knowledge over the course of their lifetimes." In other words, we want **students to develop a love of words so that they can become more motivated to independently search out richer, more precise vocabulary words beyond the classroom.**

For years, research in the area of vocabulary instruction was seemingly at a standstill. Since the publication of the National Reading Panel's (NRP) report in 2000 identifying key methods and skills that are important for reading achievement, vocabulary instruction is once again receiving the attention it deserves from educators. **For beginning readers, vocabulary plays a vital role in reading achievement.** As the research suggests, having a large vocabulary is correlated with success in school; conversely, having a small vocabulary is associated with performing poorly in school (Anderson & Nagy 1993). The vocabulary disparity between students with poor vocabularies versus rich vocabularies increases each year (Baker, Simmons, & Kameenui 1995). Researchers' estimates of how many vocabulary words per day students can learn varies widely, with an average number of seven words being most commonly cited (Beck, McKeown, & Kucan 2002). This number does not represent the number of vocabulary words learned by at-risk students who may be learning fewer words than this. In addition, the limited vocabulary of English language learners (ELL) puts them at risk of poor school performance in reading, in participation in the academic routines in the classroom, and in the development of social interactions with peers (Blachowicz, Fisher, & Watts-Taffe 2005). ELL students would benefit from vocabulary instruction that includes both basic and more sophisticated types of vocabulary words. Thus, providing avenues of instruction in which students have an equal opportunity to develop larger, richer vocabularies is important.

In *Put Reading First: the Research Building Blocks for Teaching Children to Read* developed by the Center for the Improvement of Early Reading Achievement (CIERA) in 2001 and funded by the National Institute for Literacy (NIFL), the authors note that much of a child's vocabulary development is learned **indirectly** through their everyday experiences with language, both oral and written. **As teachers, we can foster an environment in which indirect vocabulary learning**

#50700   *Early Childhood Vocabulary Development Activities*

takes place by encouraging conversations **with our students, by reading aloud** to our students often, and by encouraging students to **read extensively on their own.** It has been noted that **children in the early grades learn approximately 3,000 new words each year,** and that attempting to teach this many words directly to students would be impossible (Baker, et al, 1995). There is, however, the need for **direct vocabulary instruction** as well. In direct instruction planning, the focus should be on three types of words (CIERA 2001):

- important words that are necessary to understand a concept
- useful words that students are likely to see repeatedly
- difficult words or phrases such as idioms and multi-meaning words

This book can be used in conjunction with any language arts program that you are currently using. Your students will enjoy the activities in this book and will develop an interest in the words that surround their everyday lives.

How to Use This Book

Selecting Games and Activities

The titles of each of the activities and games in this book are listed in the table of contents along with the skills covered in each lesson. Begin by reviewing the list of activities and games by the skill you want to teach to your students. Then refer to the "Activity Procedure" section of each lesson for an overview of how the lesson will be presented to students. Many of the activities and games throughout this book can be adapted to other skills listed in the table of contents. For example, the memory game found in the "Packing List" lesson can be adapted for use with almost any of the vocabulary lists found in the remaining activities.

Preparation and Storage

The materials needed for each activity or game are listed on the teacher direction pages. Specific patterns or vocabulary word cards that may be needed are on the pages following the teacher directions. The patterns and word cards can be photocopied in black and white from this book and then colored by hand, or they can be **printed in full color from the interactive whiteboard-compatible Teacher Resource CD**. Glue the pieces to construction paper or thin cardstock to create more durable materials. Consider laminating all the materials for durability, too. Enlarging the materials is another option you may wish to consider. Use a copy machine with an enlarge option, or copy the pattern onto a transparency. Place the transparency on an overhead projector, and trace the image onto a piece of poster board.

A 9" x 12" (23 cm x 30 cm) manila envelope with a clasp works well to store most of the materials needed for each game. You may want to create an envelope for each game in order to keep the pieces organized and easy to access. Be sure to clearly label each envelope with the name of the activity. Once the necessary materials are gathered, preparation for the activities is minimal. Consider photocopying the teacher direction page and cutting out the "Activity Procedures." Glue this box to the front of the manila envelope. These directions tell how to do the activity or play the game. The envelope can be handed to a parent volunteer or classroom aide. Minimal verbal directions will be needed because everything needed is contained within the envelope.

How to Use This Book
(cont.)

Introducing the Activities and Games

Even though some of the lessons are designed for a small group, you may wish to introduce the activities in a whole-class setting. You may want to select a few students to help you demonstrate how to do the activity or play the game, or you may be able to modify the activity slightly in order to accommodate the whole class. An overhead projector, document camera, or interactive whiteboard are other methods of introducing an activity to the whole class. Photocopy necessary patterns or word cards onto transparencies, which can then be projected on a screen for the whole class to see.

The activities can also be introduced in a small-group setting. Be sure to consistently describe and play any of the games with each group to which you introduce them. When the children play the game independent of teacher supervision, you want them to all play by the same rules. In order to decide the best method of introduction for your students, consider your class and the particular activity. It is useful to remind students each time an activity is introduced that the purpose is to learn new vocabulary words, not to see who can win. You may wish to make it a policy that everyone gets a sticker, "kudos" from the teacher, or any other small prize if they participate in the activity. This reinforces the idea that everyone is a winner when the focus is on learning new vocabulary words.

Many of the activities involve the use of a pocket chart to place vocabulary word cards for students to see. If a pocket chart is unavailable, there are a few other options. The *Laundry Day* activity (page 22) uses yarn as a clothesline from which the vocabulary word cards are hung with clothespins or paper clips. This clothesline idea is a simple alternative to using a pocket chart. A classroom bulletin board that can be used during instruction would be another location for hanging up the word cards. Finally, arts and crafts stores sell rolls of magnet tape. One side of the tape has a sticky backing that will adhere to the back of the word cards. Just cut off a piece of magnet tape about 1 inch (2.5 cm) long for each card. The other side of the tape will stick to any metal surface. This tape will stick to many dry-erase boards. The vocabulary words can be hung on the dry-erase board for easy placement and have the advantage of being easy to move around during word-sort activities.

How to Use This Book (cont.)

Parent Volunteers and Classroom Aides

Utilize parent volunteers and classroom aides to assist you in preparing the materials in this book. Often, parents who are unable to volunteer in the classroom are willing to assist in coloring or assembling materials that are sent home. Be sure to provide directions and all the materials necessary for the volunteers to complete the task. Providing a "return by" date also helps you get the materials back in a timely manner.

Parent volunteers, classroom aides, and cross-age tutors are excellent resources to monitor small groups as they play games. Provide any volunteers with directions on how the activity is to be done. Remind the volunteers that the purpose of the activity is to practice using new vocabulary words.

Who Goes First?

Who goes first? This is probably one of the most hotly contested questions when children play games. You will want to have this question answered prior to introducing an activity or game to your students. You may wish to have a set procedure that can be used for determining who goes first for all activities, or you may wish to select a different procedure for each activity. Either way, having the procedure established will eliminate many arguments. Some suggestions for determining who goes first are listed below.

- Roll a die
- Draw straws
- Pull numbers out of a hat or other container
- Flip a coin
- Play "Rock, Paper, Scissors"
- Select the person wearing the most blue clothing (or any other color)
- Choose the youngest/oldest
- Ladies first/gentlemen first

Related Books

At the end of the teacher directions section for each lesson is a list of possible read-aloud books related to the topic. These books provide opportunities to introduce the topic, enrich the lesson, or provide students with further interactions with the vocabulary words. You may want to look for any of these books at your school's library or public library before introducing an activity to the students.

Because the research indicates the need for ongoing review of introduced vocabulary words, creating a way to "collect" rich vocabulary words in the classroom is important. The ideas are simple yet effective ways to keep vocabulary words that have been introduced to students accessible throughout the school year.

Beyond the Book

The Word Jar

Donovan's Word Jar by Monalisa DeGross (1994) is a wonderful chapter book about a young boy who collects words in a jar. Once the jar becomes filled, he searches for new ideas for collecting his beloved words. In the end, he realizes that sharing the words with others brings greater joy than keeping them in a container for himself.

Donovan's Word Jar is a wonderful springboard for introducing the idea of collecting rich vocabulary words in the classroom. Graves and Watts-Taffe's (2002) idea of promoting classroom environments in which children develop an awareness and an interest in new words can be implicitly taught by creating a class word jar. Draw the outline of a jar on a large piece of butcher paper, and cut out the shape. Place the new word jar on a bulletin board. After introducing a new vocabulary word to the students, write the word on an index card, and pin it on the word jar for students to refer to later.

Moore and Lyon (2005) summarized the research for teaching individual words. Using this six-step strategy before adding a word to the word jar can help students increase their vocabulary development.

1. Select a word from a high-quality read-aloud book that you have just finished reading to the class. See the "Works Cited" section (page 169) or the "Recommended Books" list (pages 170–171) for books referred to throughout this book, or look for a list of topic-specific books at the end of the teacher direction section for each activity. Refer to the selected word in context by rereading the sentence in which the word is found.

2. Have students say the word aloud.

3. Explain the meaning of the word to the students.

4. Give examples of other contexts in which the word may be used.

5. Ask the students to use the word in a context that is meaningful to them.

6. Have the students repeat the word.

Beyond the Book
(cont.)

Picture Dictionary

Use the "Picture Dictionary Template" (page 172) and the "Picture Dictionary Cover Template" (page 173) to create individual picture dictionaries for students. Make enough photocopies for each student to have 15 dictionary pages in his or her book. Make one photocopy of the cover for each student using 9" x 12" (23 cm x 30 cm) construction paper. Staple the dictionary pages inside the cover. Students write a vocabulary word in each space and then illustrate the word to show their understanding of its meaning.

Picture dictionaries have a variety of uses. A dictionary can be created for terms introduced in one of the content areas. For example, a math dictionary can be used to write and illustrate math vocabulary (e.g., triangle, square, circle, corner, side). Students can also use a picture dictionary to collect words from the class word jar. Picture dictionaries may also be used for collections of words that individual students find throughout their personal reading time.

Quarter It

Quarter It is a quick and easy way to have students focus on one vocabulary word that may come up during shared reading or read-aloud time. This activity can also be used in conjunction with any of the vocabulary words introduced during the activities in this book. Give each student a copy of the Quarter It template (page 174). Have them write a selected vocabulary word in the first box. Brainstorm an age-appropriate definition for the selected word, and have students write the word in the second box. Have students draw an appropriate picture for the word in the third box. In the final box, have students write a sentence using the word. You may want to have the class come up with one sentence for all the students to copy.

Once *Quarter It* is used a few times in the classroom, it becomes routine for the students. This is a wonderful activity for vocabulary development when there are only a few minutes of time to spare in class. You can also teach the students to make their own *Quarter It* page by folding a piece of 8½" x 11" (22 cm x 28 cm) paper in half, and then folding it in half again so that the paper is divided into fourths when unfolded. This saves time if you do not want to photocopy the template each time a new word is introduced.

Standards Correlations

Standards Correlations

Shell Education is committed to producing educational materials that are research and standards based. In this effort, we have correlated all of our products to the academic standards of all 50 states, the District of Columbia, and the Department of Defense Dependent Schools.

How to Find Standards Correlations

To print a customized correlation report of this product for your state, visit our website at **http://www.shelleducation.com** and follow the on-screen directions. If you require assistance in printing correlation reports, please contact Customer Service at 1-877-777-3450.

Purpose and Intent of Standards

The No Child Left Behind legislation mandates that all states adopt academic standards that identify the skills students will learn in kindergarten through grade twelve. While many states had already adopted academic standards prior to NCLB, the legislation set requirements to ensure the standards were detailed and comprehensive.

Standards are designed to focus instruction and guide adoption of curricula. Standards are statements that describe the criteria necessary for students to meet specific academic goals. They define the knowledge, skills, and content students should acquire at each level. Standards are also used to develop standardized tests to evaluate students' academic progress.

Teachers are required to demonstrate how their lessons meet state standards. State standards are used in development of all of our products, so educators can be assured they meet the academic requirements of each state.

McREL Compendium

We use the Mid-continent Research for Education and Learning (McREL) Compendium to create standards correlations. Each year, McREL analyzes state standards and revises the compendium. By following this procedure, McREL is able to produce a general compilation of national standards. Each lesson in this product is based on one or more McREL standards. The chart on the following page lists each standard taught in this product and the page numbers for the corresponding lessons.

Standards Correlation Chart

Subject and Standard	Benchmark	Lesson and Page Numbers
Language Arts **Standard 5** Uses the general skills and strategies of the reading process	**Standard 5.6 Level K-2** Understands level-appropriate sight words and vocabulary (e.g., words for places, things, actions; high frequency words such as *said, was, and, where*)	Packing List..................................14–21 Going Places............................ 32–37 Moving Day.............................. 52–57 Home Sweet Home.................. 92–97 School Supplies......................118–123 School Bell .... 124–127 Musical Movements...............136–141 Odd Man Out.........................142–149
Language Arts **Standard 8** Uses listening and speaking strategies for different purposes	**Standard 8.2 Level Pre-K** Uses new vocabulary to describe feelings, thoughts, experiences, and observations	Maggie's First Day 98–103
	Standard 8.4 Level Pre-K Uses descriptive language (e.g., color words; size words, such as bigger, smaller; shape words)	Laundry Day............................... 22–27 Shapeosaurus............................. 44–51 Size 'Em Up................................ 66–71
	Standard 8.5 Level K-2 Uses level-appropriate vocabulary in speech (e.g., number words; words that describe people, places, things, events, location, actions; synonyms, homonyms, word analogies, common figures of speech)	Laundry Day............................. 22–27 A Pair of Socks ....28–31 Shapeosaurus.............................44–51 Rolling for Opposites .... 58–65 Size 'Em Up................................. 66–71 Don't Bug Me! ....72–75 Don't Spill the Beans................82–91 Maggie's First Day ....98–103 Handshakes............................104–111 Compound Clues ....112–117 Build a Weather Bear ....128–135 Using My Senses....................150–168

Standards Correlation Chart

Subject and Standard	Benchmark	Lesson and Page Numbers
Mathematics Standard 5 Understands and applies basic and advanced properties of the concepts of geometry	**Standard 5.1 Level Pre-K** Knows basic geometric language for naming shapes (e.g., circle, triangle, square, rectangle)	Shapeosaurus..........................44–51
	Standard 5.2 Level K-2 Understands the common language of spatial sense (e.g., left, right, horizontal, in front of)	Flies, Flies Everywhere! ....38–43 Going on a Treasure Hunt 76–81
	Standard 8.1 Level Pre-K Knows vocabulary used to describe some observable properties (e.g., color, shape, size) of objects	Laundry Day.........................22–27 Shapeosaurus........................44–51 Size 'Em Up..........................66–71
Science Standard 8 Understands the structures and property of matter	**Standard 8.1 Level K-2** Knows that different objects are made up of many different types of materials (e.g., cloth, paper, wood, metal) and have many different observable properties (e.g., color, size, shape, weight)	Laundry Day.........................22–27 Shapeosaurus........................44–51

Packing List

Skill:

Recognizing clothing words

Suggested Group Size:

Small group (6–12 students)

Activity Overview:

Students play a cumulative memory game by listing clothing items that can be packed in a suitcase for a make-believe trip.

Materials:

- "Clothing Cards–Set A" (pages 16–18)
- a suitcase (optional)

Vocabulary Words:

Set A

blouse	shirt
boots	shoes
coat	shorts
hat	skirt
pajamas	socks
pants	sweater

Activity Preparation

1. Photocopy "Clothing Cards–Set A" onto cardstock paper and color as desired (or print color copies from the CD).
2. Cut out the cards.
3. Laminate the cards for durability.

Building Background

Have the students sit on the floor in a circle. Explain to the students that you are going on a trip and will need to pack some clothing items in your suitcase. Show the students a suitcase if you have one available. Tell the students that you will need their help to remember what to pack.

Activity Procedure

1. Pass out one card facedown from "Clothing Cards–Set A" to each student so that only the student holding each card can see the picture. There may be extra cards, depending on the number of students that will be playing.

2. Have the first student to your left show his or her card to the class and say, "Don't forget to pack (say name of the picture) in the suitcase" (e.g., "Don't forget to pack a *shirt* in the suitcase.").

3. Tell the next student in the circle to show his or her card and repeat what the previous student stated, adding the item pictured on his or her card to the list. (e.g., "Don't forget to pack a *shirt* and a *vest* in the suitcase.").

4. Continue the game with each student taking turns showing a card and listing not only his or her pictured clothing item, but all of the previous items listed by the students who have had a turn (e.g., "Don't forget to pack a *shirt*, a *vest*, a *tie*, *pants*, *socks*...in the suitcase."). If you are using all 12 vocabulary cards, then the final student to play will list all 12 words in the sentence! For support, the "Clothing Cards" are always available for the students to look at if an item is forgotten.

Adaptations

- Use cards from set A and set B (pages 19–20) if you want to do the activity with more than 12 students. There are 20 cards in both sets combined.

- Challenge the students to create hand gestures to symbolize the clothing items after they receive their "Clothing Cards." Instead of showing the picture cards to classmates, each student will show the related hand gesture to help classmates remember the items on the list.

- Discuss different types of clothing that come in pairs.

- Have the students sort all 20 cards in different ways (e.g., items worn on the feet, items worn on the head, etc.). As an independent activity, the students can complete the "Clothing Sort" (page 21) by writing or drawing vocabulary words in the appropriate categories.

Related Books

The Spiffiest Giant in Town by Julia Donaldson

The Skeleton in the Closet by Alice Schertle

blouse

boots

coat

hat

pajamas

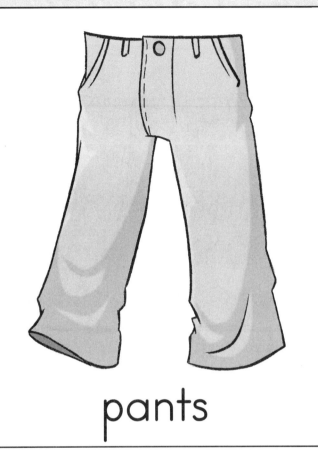

pants

shirt

shoes

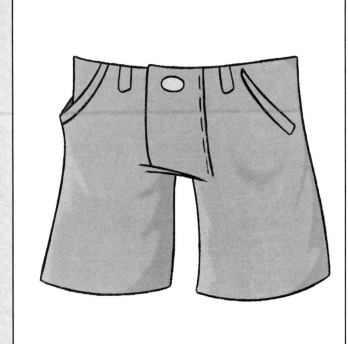

shorts

skirt

socks

sweater

bathing suit

belt

jacket

sandals

scarf

slippers

tie

vest

Clothing Sort

I would *not* wear these clothes in winter.

I would *wear* these clothes in winter.

Laundry Day

Skill:

Identifying color words

Suggested Group Size:

Whole class

Activity Overview:

Students match T-shirts of various colors with their corresponding color word cards.

Materials:

- "T-Shirt Cards" (page 24)
- "Color Word Cards" (pages 25–27)
- 10 feet (approx. 3 meters) of yarn
- 22 clothespins or paper clips

Vocabulary Words:

red	pink
yellow	brown
blue	black
green	white
purple	gray
orange	

Activity Preparation

1. Photocopy three copies of "T-Shirt Cards" onto cardstock paper, and color each shirt a different color selected from the vocabulary list (or print color copies from the CD).
2. Photocopy "Color Word Cards" onto cardstock paper, and color the words in the corresponding color (or print color copies from the CD).
3. Cut out the cards, and laminate them for durability.
4. Suspend the yarn horizontally about five feet (1.5 meters) from the floor. This will be the clothesline.
5. Hang the "T-Shirt Cards" on one half of the clothesline using clothespins or paper clips. Leave room for the "Color Word Cards" on the other half of the clothesline. All cards should be facing away from the students so that they cannot see the color on the front.

Building Background

Ask the students if any of them have ever helped wash clothes at home. Tell the students that on laundry day, some people will hang their just-washed clothing on a clothesline to dry. Show the students the "clothesline" that was pre-hung and explain that they will be playing a color matching game using the clothesline with color word cards and picture cards.

Activity Procedure

1. Review the vocabulary words using the "Color Word Cards."

2. Mix up the cards and hang them up on the clothesline so that they are facing away from the students.

3. Select a student to come up to the clothesline, and point to any of the "T-Shirt Cards." Flip the card over so that the colored T-shirt is now showing.

4. Have the same student point to any of the "Color Word Cards." Flip that card over as well. If the "Color Word Card" and the "T-Shirt Card" match, then that student may keep the two cards and return to his or her seat. If the two cards do not match, the cards are flipped back so they cannot be seen.

5. Have other students take turns following the same procedure. The game is over when all of the cards have been removed from the clothesline.

Adaptations

- Make enough sets of this game for students to work in groups of two to four children. They can lay out the cards on the floor or a table instead of hanging the cards from a clothesline.

- Select a color not on the list, and color in an extra "T-Shirt Card" with that color. Tell the students that this is a mystery color. Have them guess what the name of the color is, and write the correct answer on the back of the blank "Color Word Card."

Related Books

The Crayon Box That Talked by Shane DeRolf

A Rainbow All Around Me by Sandra Pinkney

My World of Color by Margaret Wise Brown

T-Shirt Cards

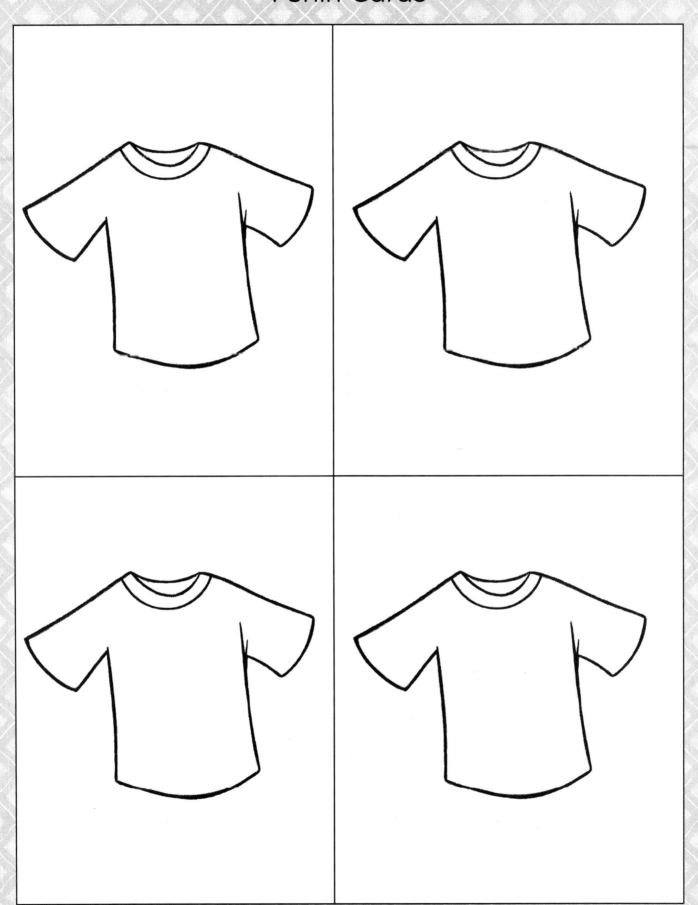

#50700   *Early Childhood Vocabulary Development Activities*

Color Word Cards

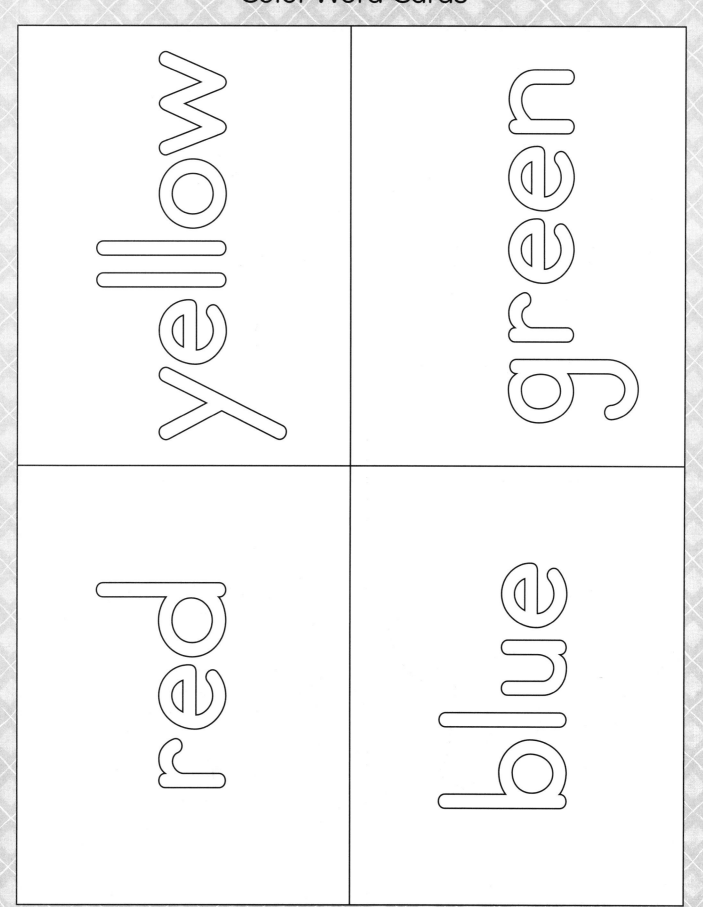

yellow

green

red

blue

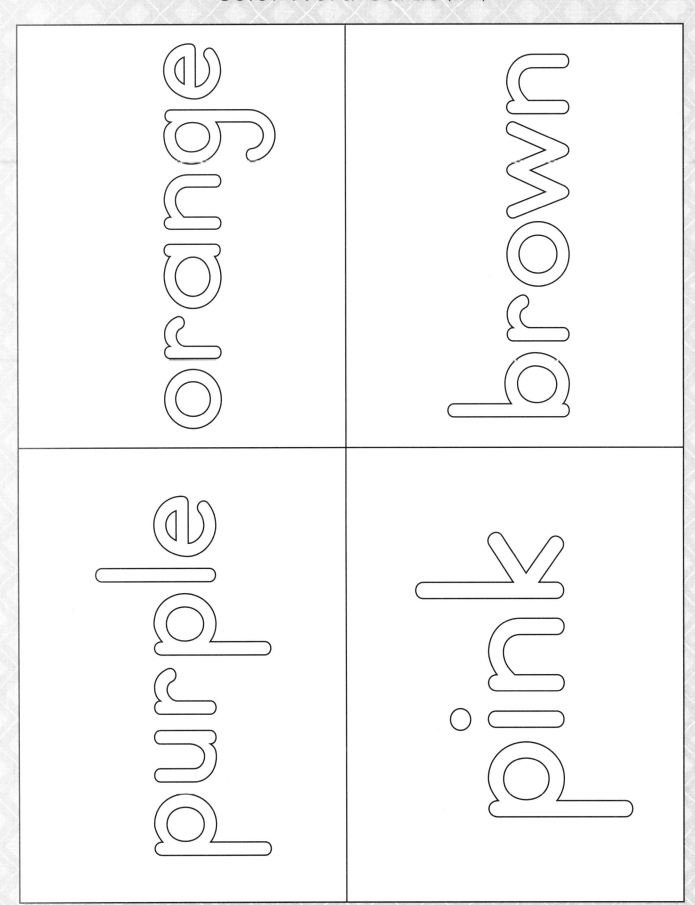

orange

brown

purple

pink

#50700   Early Childhood Vocabulary Development Activities

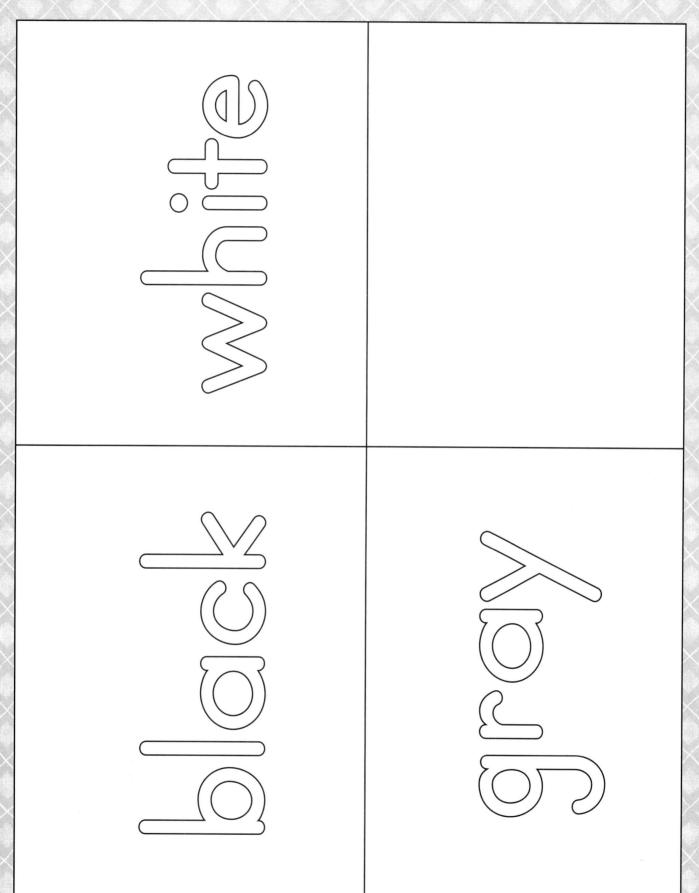

white

black

gray

A Pair of Socks

Skill:

Recognizing homophones

Suggested Group Size:

Small group (6–8 students)

Activity Overview:

Students will work with partners to draw pictures of selected pairs of homophones.

Materials:

- "Pairs of Socks Cards" (page 30)
- "Cover Page" (page 31)
- "Book Page" (page 175)
- crayons

Vocabulary Words:

two	to
knight	night
sea	see
pear	pair
won	one

Activity Preparation

1. Photocopy five copies of "Pairs of Socks Cards" onto cardstock paper, and color as desired (or print color copies from the CD). If you are coloring the socks, each pair of socks should be a different color than the other nine pairs.
2. Write one of the vocabulary words on the back of each sock. Each pair of homophones should be written on matching colored socks.
3. Cut out the cards, and laminate them for durability.
4. Make four copies of "Book Page," one for each pair of students to share.

Building Background

Ask the students to tell a partner what the word *pair* means. Have the students share their answers. Show the students the two "Pairs of Socks Cards" with the words *pair* and *pear*. Explain that some words sound the same as others but are spelled differently and have totally different meanings. Discuss the meanings for the words *pair* and *pear*.

Activity Procedure

1. Mix up the remaining eight "Pairs of Socks Cards." Pass out one card to each student. Have the students walk around the room, and find a partner who has a matching color sock. Once all the students have found their partners, have them sit down on the floor next to their partners.

2. Bring up each pair of students along with the matching color socks to the front of the class. Have the students read aloud the homophones written on their pairs of socks or read the words for them. Discuss the meaning of each word. Ask the students to decide what kind of picture they could draw to represent their homophones. Repeat this procedure with the remaining pairs of students.

3. Distribute one "Book Page" to each pair of students. Have them work together to complete the page by writing each word from their pair of socks on the writing lines and illustrating them as well.

4. When all the students have finished, collect all the pages and bind them together to make a class book. Use the "Cover Page" for the cover of the book.

Adaptations

- Adapt the activity for a class of 20 students by making 10 copies of the "Pairs of Socks Cards" and extra copies of the "Book Page." Make up other homophones for students to use or use the following pairs of words: *ate, eight; blew, blue; hair, hare; hear, here; right, write; toe, tow.*

- Make extra copies of the "Book Page." If the students find other examples of homophones throughout the year, they can make a new page for the class book.

- Create sentences using pairs of homophones from the class book.

Related Books

Eight Ate: A Feast of Homonym Riddles by Marvin Terban

A Chocolate Moose for Dinner by Fred Gwynne

The King Who Rained by Fred Gwynne

Pairs of Socks Cards

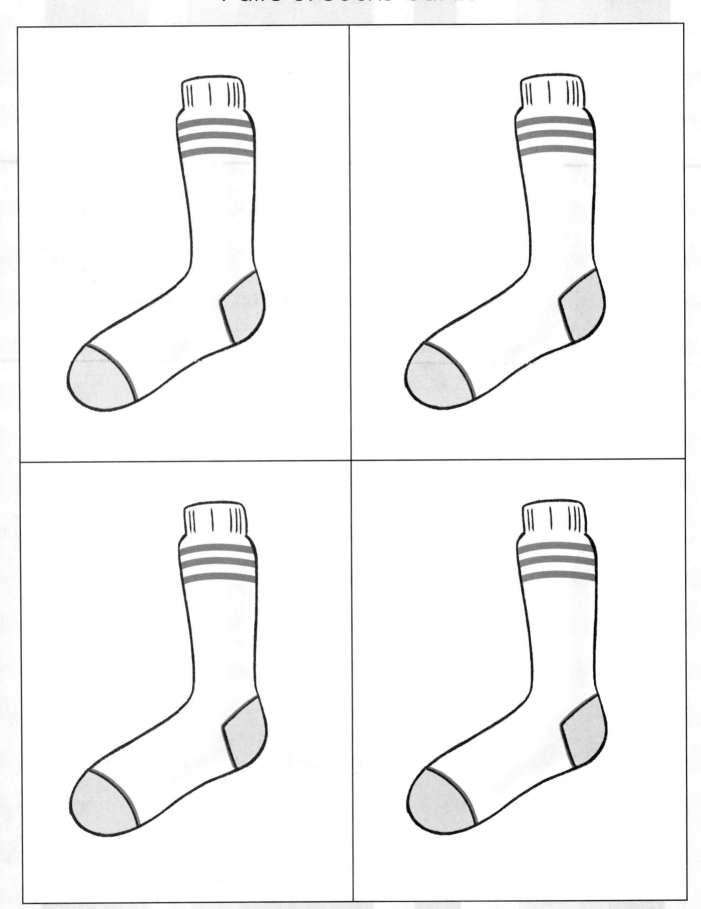

#50700   *Early Childhood Vocabulary Development Activities*

Our Class Book

of

Homophones

Going Places

Skill:

Recognizing types of transportation

Suggested Group Size:

Small group (2–4 students)

Activity Overview:

Students will discuss types of transportation and sort them by different characteristics.

Materials:

- "Transportation Cards–Set A" (pages 34–35)
- envelopes for each set of cards
- chart paper and marker
- pocket chart

Vocabulary Words:

Set A

airplane	helicopter
bicycle	sailboat
bus	ship
car	train

Activity Preparation

1. Photocopy two sets of "Transportation Cards–Set A" onto cardstock paper, and color one set as desired (or print color copies from the CD). You will need the colored set for instruction, plus a set of cards for the small group.

2. Cut out the cards, and laminate them for durability.

3. Store each set of cards in a separate envelope.

Building Background

Ask the students to share vacation experiences and how they got to their destinations. Make a list on chart paper of the types of transportation that are mentioned. Explain that today they will be learning about many different types of transportation. Define transportation as something that can get you from one place to another.

Activity Procedure

1. Show the colored "Transportation Cards" one at a time to the students, allowing them to share what they know about each one. After each word is introduced, place the card in a pocket chart.

2. Pass out a set of "Transportation Cards" to the group. Allow time for the students to look at and discuss their cards. Explain to the students that they will be working together in their groups to sort their cards. Show the students how to lay out all of the cards in two rows on the table before they begin each round. Read the directions for one round and allow time for the students to sort their cards before moving on to the next round.

   - Round 1: Sort into two groups—*things that fly* and *things that do not fly*
   - Round 2: Sort into two groups—*things that travel on water* and *things that do not*
   - Round 3: Sort into two groups—*things that can carry more than 20 people* and *things that cannot*
   - Round 4: Sort into two groups—*things a family can use to get to the grocery store* and *things a family would not use*
   - Round 5: Sort into two groups—*things a family can use to travel from the United States to Australia* and *things a family would not use*
   - Round 6: Sort into three groups—*things that travel on land, things that travel in the air,* and *things that travel on the water*

Adaptations

- Adapt the activity for more of a challenge by including "Transportation Cards–Set B" (pages 36-37) with the previous set of cards. Set B includes the following words: *cable car, canoe, motorboat, motorcycle, space shuttle, subway, truck,* and *van*.

- Make overhead transparencies of "Transportation Cards," and cut them out. You may want to shrink the "Transportation Cards" masters first so that the cards are a more manageable size. Have the students take turns coming up to the overhead projector to sort the cards in front of the class.

Related Books

Zip, Whiz, Zoom! by Stephanie Calmenson

Choo Choo Clickety-Clack! by Margaret Mayo

How We Travel by Rebecca Weber

GO! by Daniel Kirk

Transportation Cards–Set A

airplane

bicycle

bus

car

#50700   *Early Childhood Vocabulary Development Activities*

helicopter

sailboat

ship

train

Transportation Cards–Set B

cable car

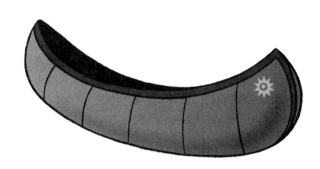

canoe

motorboat

motorcycle

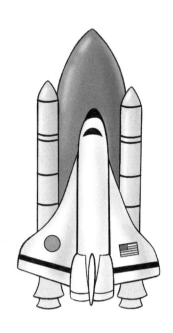

space shuttle

subway

truck

van

Flies, Flies Everywhere!

Skill:

Using words to describe location

Suggested Group Size:

Whole class or small group

Activity Overview:

Students will use location words to describe where a fly finger puppet can be found.

Materials:

- "Flies, Flies Everywhere! Chant" (page 40)
- "Fly Finger Puppet" (page 41)
- "Location Word Cards" (pages 42–43)
- glue or transparent tape
- pocket chart

Vocabulary Words:

above	far from
behind	on
below	to the left of
beside	to the right of

Activity Preparation

1. Photocopy "Fly Finger Puppet" and "Location Word Cards" onto cardstock paper, (or print color copies from the CD). You will only need one of the two flies for this activity.
2. Cut out the cards and laminate them for durability.
3. Put together a finger puppet as directed on the "Fly Finger Puppet" master.
4. Place the "Location Word Cards" in a pocket chart so that each card is facing away from the students.
5. Make a poster of "Flies, Flies Everywhere! Chant" or make an overhead transparency.

Building Background

Pretend that you see a fly buzzing around the room. Tell the students to look for the fly. Explain that sometimes when it is difficult to find something, we need to use special words to describe where something can be found. Show the students the paper fly, and explain that they will be learning special location words to describe where the fly is by playing a game called "Flies, Flies Everywhere!"

Activity Procedure

1. Review the vocabulary on the "Location Word Cards" with the students.

2. Teach the students the "Flies, Flies Everywhere!" chant. Tell them to point to the fly puppet whenever they say the last word of the chant during the game.

3. Select a student to sit in front of the class. Choose another student to start the game by handing him or her the fly finger puppet. The student then flies the puppet up to the pocket chart and selects a location word card. The student hands the card to you. Read the card aloud to the class, or have the class read it to you. The chosen student then flies the puppet to the student sitting in front of the class and makes the fly hover at the location written on the location card. If the fly is correctly placed, have the students recite the chant. If the fly is incorrectly placed, give the student a hint to help him or her with the proper placement.

4. Continue the game by passing the fly finger puppet to a new student and repeating the process.

Adaptations

- Select a student to sit in a chair in front of the class. Move the fly to the sitting student so that it hovers or sits at a location indicated on any of the location cards. Choose a student from the class to decide which location word in the pocket chart matches the location of the fly.

- Instead of a student sitting in the chair, use a large stuffed animal.

- Make enough fly finger puppets for each student. Let each student use the puppet to give location directions to a partner.

Related Books

On Top of Spaghetti by Paul Johnson

Flies, Flies Everywhere!
Flies, flies
Everywhere,
On the ground
And in the air.
Flies, flies
Everywhere,
We can see one
Sitting there!

Fly Finger Puppet

Cut out the fly and rectangle. Make a band out of the rectangle just large enough to fit around your finger. Tape or glue the band together. Tape the band to the back of the fly.

Cut out the fly and rectangle. Make a band out of the rectangle just large enough to fit around your finger. Tape or glue the band together. Tape the band to the back of the fly.

above

behind

below

beside

far from

on

to the
left of

to the
right of

SHAPEOSAURUS

Skill:
Recognizing and describing shapes

Suggested Group Size:
Whole class or small group

Activity Overview:
Students will create dinosaurs using common geometric shapes and will describe the shapes used.

Materials:

- "Shape Cards" (pages 46–47)
- "Basic Shapes" (pages 48–50)
- "Shapeosaurus Sample" (page 51)
- *Patrick's Dinosaurs* by Carol Carrick (Clarion Books, 1983) or any other dinosaur book
- 9" x 12" (23 cm x 30 cm) colored construction paper, one per student
- pocket chart
- dry-erase marker
- one envelope
- scissors, glue, and crayons for each student

Vocabulary Words:

circle	rectangle
oval	pentagon
triangle	sides
square	corners

Activity Preparation

1. Photocopy "Shape Picture Cards" and the "Shapeosaurus Sample" onto cardstock paper, and color as desired (or print color copies from the CD).
2. Cut out the cards, and laminate them for durability.
3. Laminate "Shapeosaurus Sample" for durability.
4. Make one copy of "Basic Shapes" masters for each student on white copy paper and one copy for the teacher.
5. Cut out the shapes on the teacher copy of the "Basic Shapes" pages. Place the shapes in an envelope.

Building Background

Read *Patrick's Dinosaurs* or any other fun book about dinosaurs to the class. Explain to the students that they will be creating their own special dinosaurs called "shapeosauruses" using shapes that they see everyday. Show the "Shapeosaurus Sample" to the class.

#50700 *Early Childhood Vocabulary Development Activities*

Activity Procedure

1. Place the shape cards in the pocket chart one at a time. Discuss each shape with the students. Emphasize the card with the word *sides*. Select volunteers to count the number of sides there are on each shape. Write the answers on the back of each card with a dry-erase marker. Then show the students the shape card with the word *corners* written on it. Ask volunteers to count the number of corners there are on each shape. Write the answers on the back of each card with a dry-erase marker. Ask the students if they notice any patterns with the number of sides and number of corners each shape has. (The number of sides will equal the number of corners on each shape.)

2. Show the students how to use the shapes from the "Basic Shapes" page to make a unique dinosaur. Use the shapes from the teacher envelope to model how to first lay out the shapes, and then glue them onto a piece of construction paper. Tell the students that they may use crayons to add details to their pictures if they choose.

3. Pass out a copy of each "Basic Shapes" page and a piece of construction paper to each student. Tell the students that they do not need to cut out all of the shapes on the "Basic Shapes" page—just the ones that they will need to create their shapeosauruses. Explain that they should try to use at least one of each kind of shape if they can.

4. Have the students share their shapeosauruses with the class when finished. Ask each student to point out and count the number of each shape that was used (e.g., "Please point to all the triangles on your shapeosaurus and tell us how many you used.").

Adaptations

- Collect the shapeosaurus pictures. Select one picture, and show it to the class. Then select one shape card, and ask the students to count the number of times that particular shape was used in the picture.

- Play a "Name That Shape" game with the shape cards. Show the students the back of one of the cards so that the numbers of sides and corners are showing. Have them guess the name of the shape that appears on the front of the card. Continue with the remaining cards.

- Have the students draw dinosaurs. *Drawing and Learning about Dinosaurs: Using Shapes and Lines* by Amy Muehlenhardt (Picture Window Books, 2004) gives step-by-step directions using basic shapes as a basis for each drawing.

Related Books

Shape Spotters by Megan E. Bryant

Color Farm by Lois Ehlert

Shape Cards

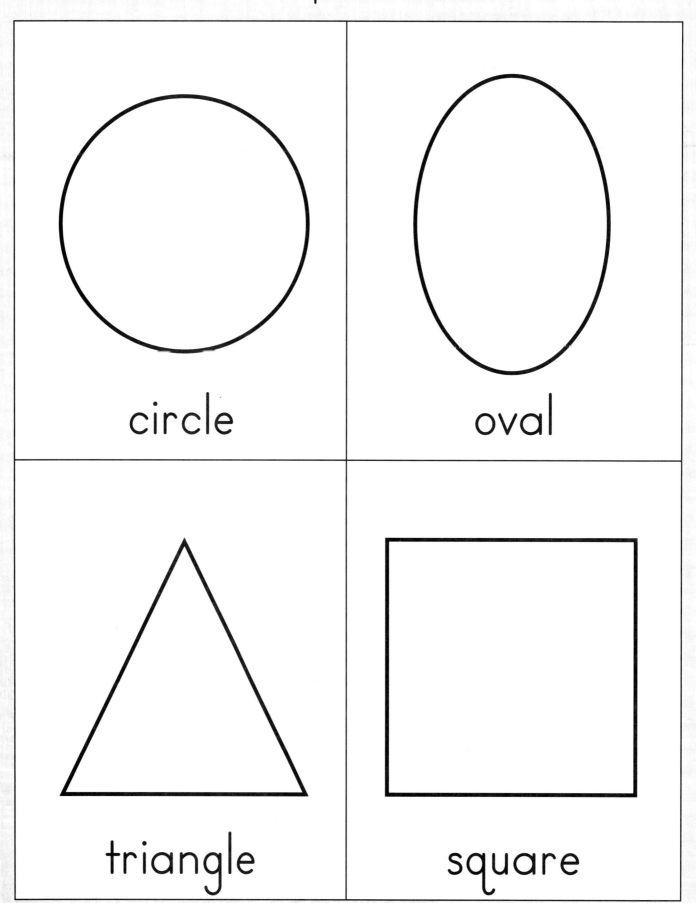

circle

oval

triangle

square

#50700   Early Childhood Vocabulary Development Activities

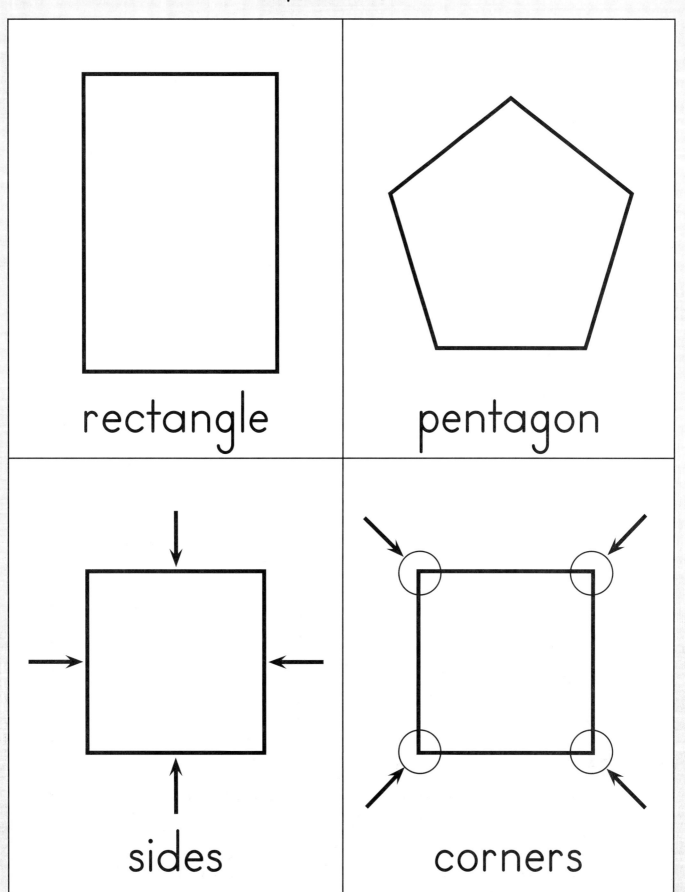

rectangle

pentagon

sides

corners

Basic Shapes

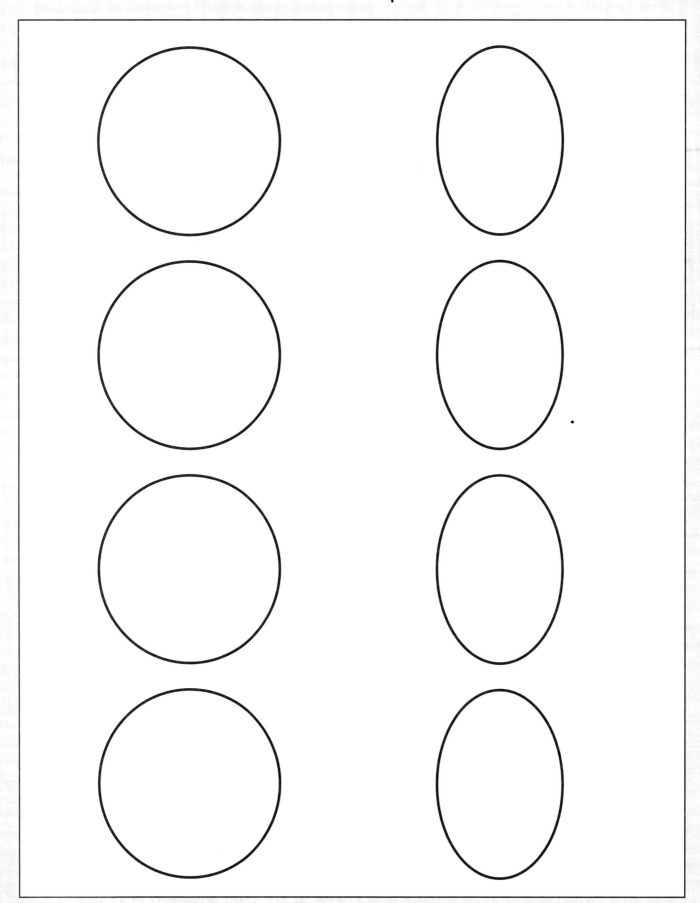

#50700   *Early Childhood Vocabulary Development Activities*   *© Shell Education*

Basic Shapes *(cont.)*

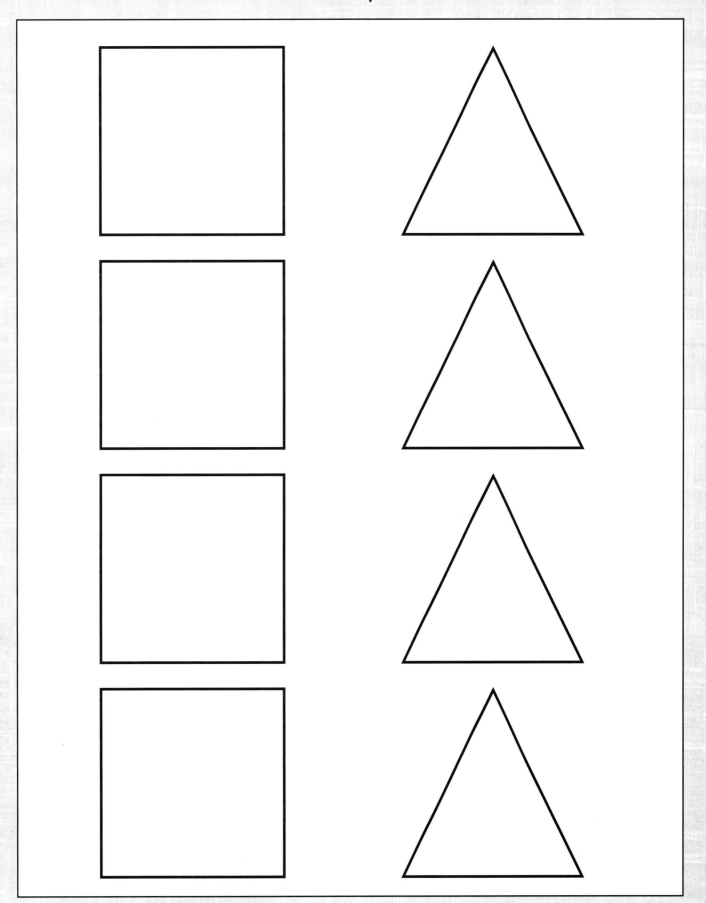

Basic Shapes (cont.)

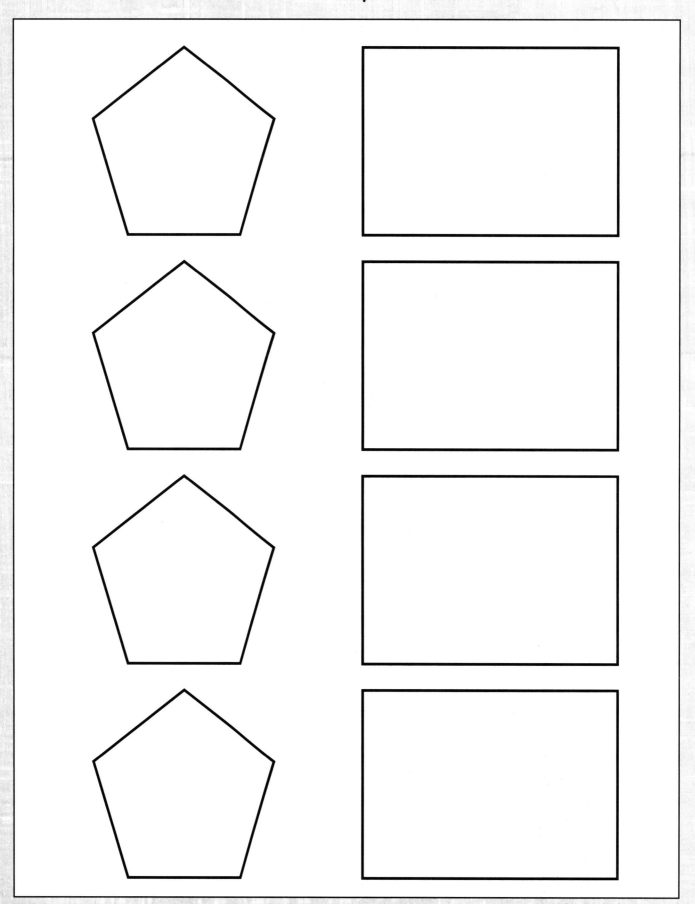

#50700   *Early Childhood Vocabulary Development Activities*

Shapeosaurus Sample

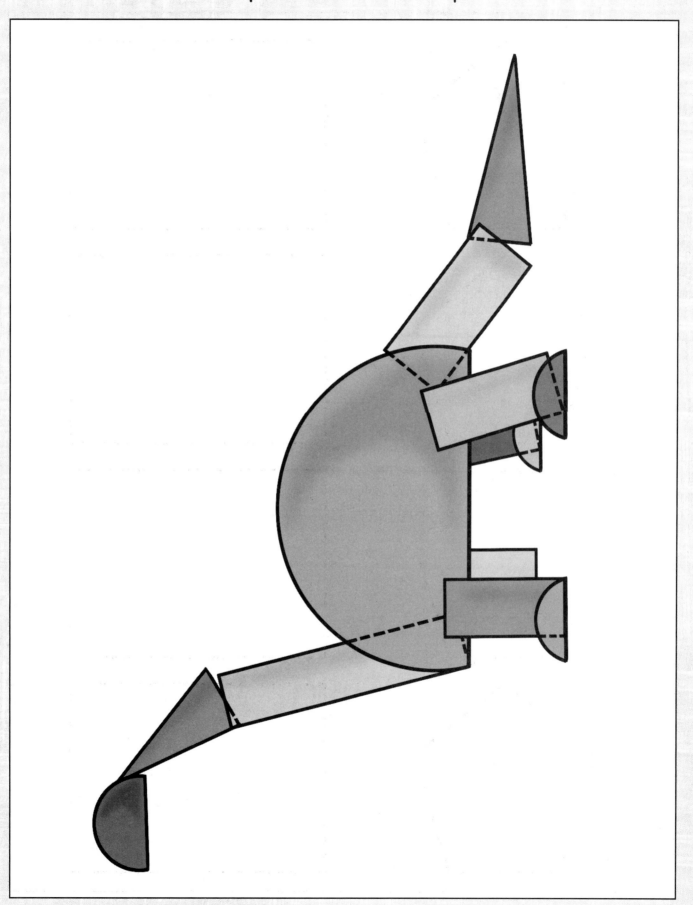

Moving Day

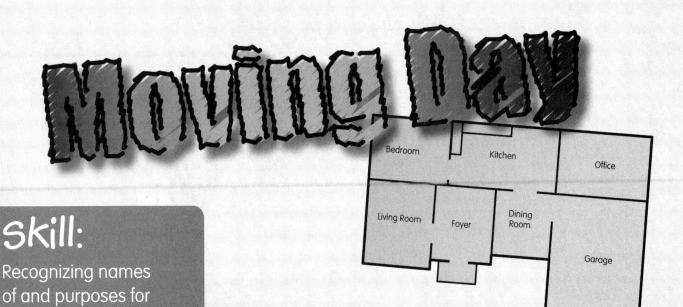

Skill:

Recognizing names of and purposes for different types of furniture

Suggested Group Size:

Small groups (6–12 students)

Activity Overview:

Students will appropriately place furniture picture cards according to their functions on a house map.

Materials:

- "House Map" (page 54)
- "Furniture Picture Cards" (pages 55–57)
- butcher paper 36" x 36" (91 cm x 91cm)
- pocket chart
- index cards
- marker
- glue

Vocabulary Words:

couch	dresser
chair	desk
stool	kitchen table
rocking chair	bed
coffee table	footstool
nightstand	bookshelf

Activity Preparation

1. Draw a large-scale map with marker onto butcher paper using "House Map" for reference. Alternatively, you can make an overhead transparency of the "House Map," and use an overhead projector to transfer the map outline onto the butcher paper with a marker.

2. Photocopy "Furniture Picture Cards" onto cardstock paper, and color as desired (or print color copies from the CD).

3. Cut out the cards, and laminate them for durability.

4. Photocopy a second set of "Furniture Picture Cards" onto white copy paper.

5. Cut out the second set of cards.

Building Background

Point to several pieces of furniture in the classroom, such as a desk, chair, or cabinet. Ask the students what each of these things has in common. Have the students brainstorm the names of other pieces of furniture. Write the word for each piece of furniture on an index card, and place the cards in a pocket chart. Then, name a room, and ask the students to use the words in the pocket chart to name all the furniture that belongs in the room you named.

Activity Procedure

1. Pretend that you have moved into a new house and you need help figuring out where to put all your furniture. Show the students the map of the house. Review the laminated set of "Furniture Picture Cards" with the students. Discuss the name for each piece of furniture, and ask the students what they think the purpose is for each piece. Leave this set out for the students to refer to during the activity.

2. Pass out the second set of "Furniture Picture Cards" to the students. Depending on the size of your group, some students may have more than one card. Have the students take turns bringing their picture cards up to the map. Each student should state the name of the piece of furniture, the room in which he or she thinks the item belongs, and the purpose for that item. The items may then be glued on the map inside the appropriate rooms.

Adaptations

■ Have blank cards available on which the students may draw other pieces of furniture to place on the diagram.

■ Ask each student to make a map of one room in his or her house, illustrating where each piece of furniture is located.

■ Ask the students if they know other possible names for each furniture card (e.g., couch, sofa, loveseat, and divan).

Related Books

Moving Day by Jo Kittinger

House Map

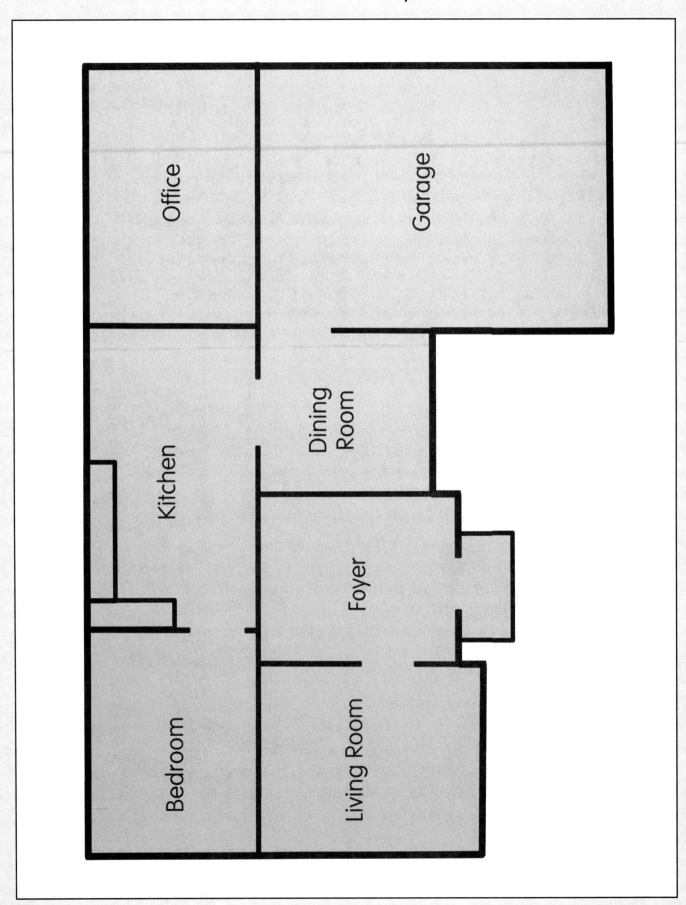

#50700   *Early Childhood Vocabulary Development Activities*

Furniture Picture Cards

couch

chair

stool

rocking chair

coffee table

nightstand

dresser

desk

kitchen table

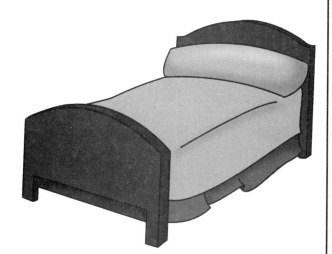

bed

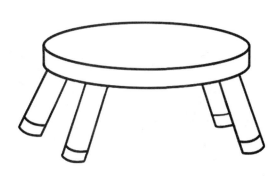

footstool

bookshelf

Rolling for Opposites

Skill:

Recognizing pairs of opposites

Suggested Group Size:

Small group (2–6 students)

Activity Overview:

Students will play a dice game asking for opposites of words listed on a die.

Materials:

- "Picture Flip Cards" (pages 60–62)
- "Die Master A" (page 63)
- "Die Master B" (page 64)
- 6 craft sticks
- glue

Vocabulary Words:

hot	cold
tall	short
up	down
fast	slow
day	night
young	old

Activity Preparation

1. Photocopy "Picture Flip Cards" onto cardstock paper, and color as desired (or print color copies from the CD).
2. Fold each card in half on the dotted line so that the picture on each side shows. Insert a craft stick between each half of the flip card so that only half of it shows, and glue shut.
3. Photocopy "Die Master A" and "Die Master B" onto cardstock paper.
4. Laminate the dice for durability.
5. Cut out the dice. Fold each die on the dotted lines. Tape or glue each die together as indicated.

Building Background

Show the students the "Picture Flip Card" that is labeled *cold*. Explain to the students that this picture shows a word that has to do with temperature. Ask for a volunteer to tell you another temperature word that is as different as possible from *cold*. Turn the card over to show the "Picture Flip Card" labeled *hot*. Explain that *cold* and *hot* both are temperature words, but they are opposites because they are very different from each other. Repeat this procedure for the other "Picture Flip Cards."

Activity Procedure

1. Tell the students that they are going to play a game called "Rolling for Opposites." Show the students one of the dice. Identify the words on all six faces. Select one student to roll the die. Read the word that is on top of the die. Have the selected student think of a word that is an opposite of the one rolled. Allow the student to use the "Picture Flip Cards" for support if necessary.

2. Repeat the procedure with the remaining students. Then, introduce the other die and continue the game.

Adaptations

- Use the "Blank Die Master" (page 65) to make another die. Add other words that are not on the vocabulary list.

- Have the students make their own "Picture Flip Cards" using the "Blank Flip Cards" master on page 176.

- Have the students work with a partner to make a page for a class "Opposites Book." Using the "Book Page" on page 175, have partners write assigned opposites on the writing lines on both halves of the paper. Then, each partner can illustrate the word on his or her half of the page.

Related Books

Big Dog, Little Dog by P.D. Eastman

This and That: Doodlezoo: A Book of Opposites by Keith Potter

Picture Flip Cards

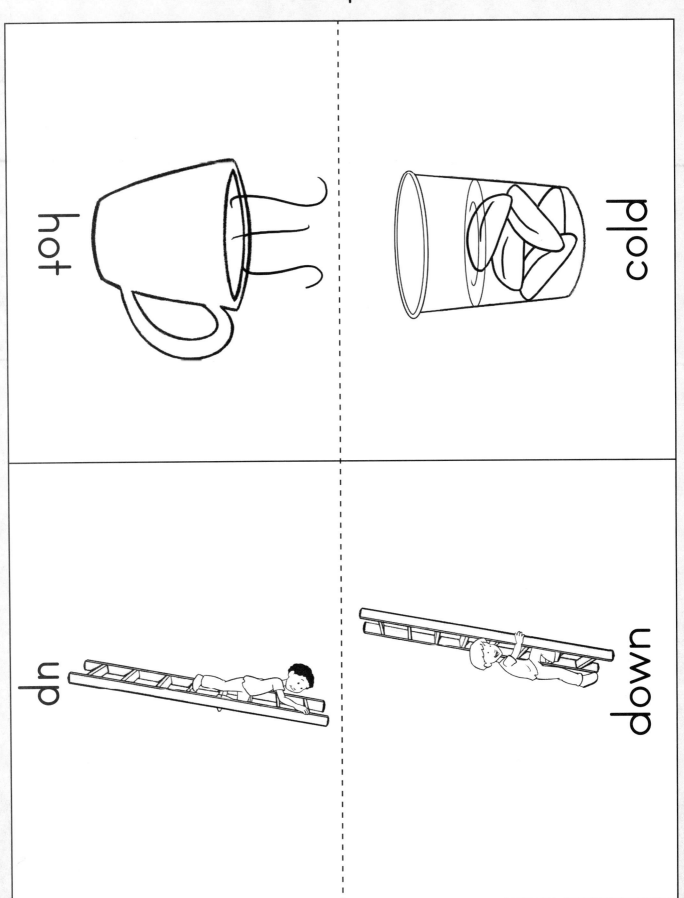

hot

cold

up

down

#50700 *Early Childhood Vocabulary Development Activities*

Picture Flip Cards *(cont.)*

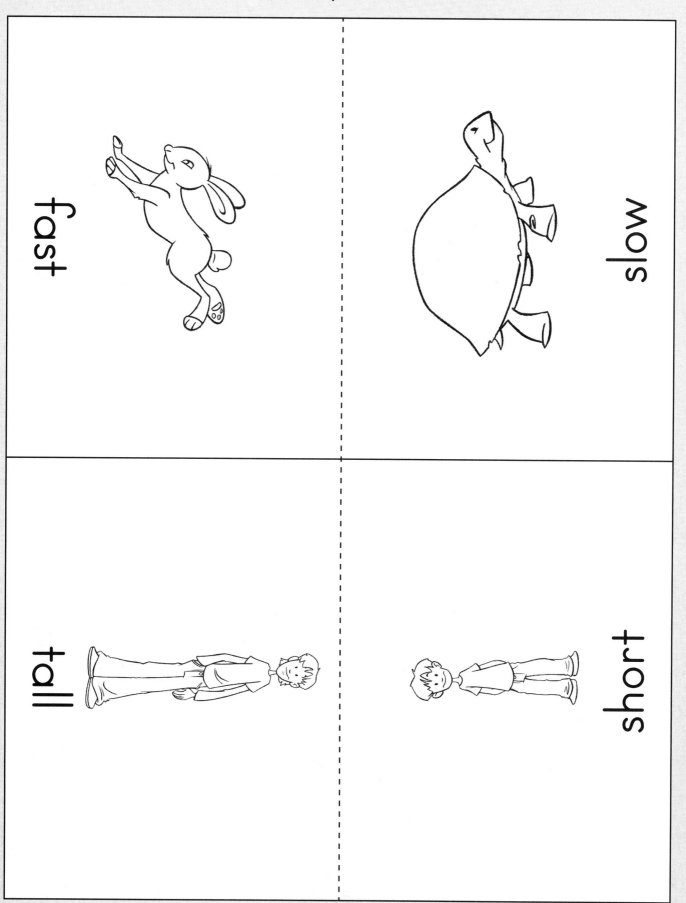

fast

slow

tall

short

Picture Flip Cards *(cont.)*

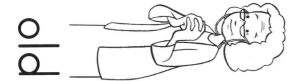

old

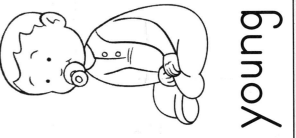

young

day

night

#50700   *Early Childhood Vocabulary Development Activities*

Die Master A

Cut along solid lines.
Fold along the dashed lines.
Tape or glue flaps to the
inside sides to create the
bottom of the box.

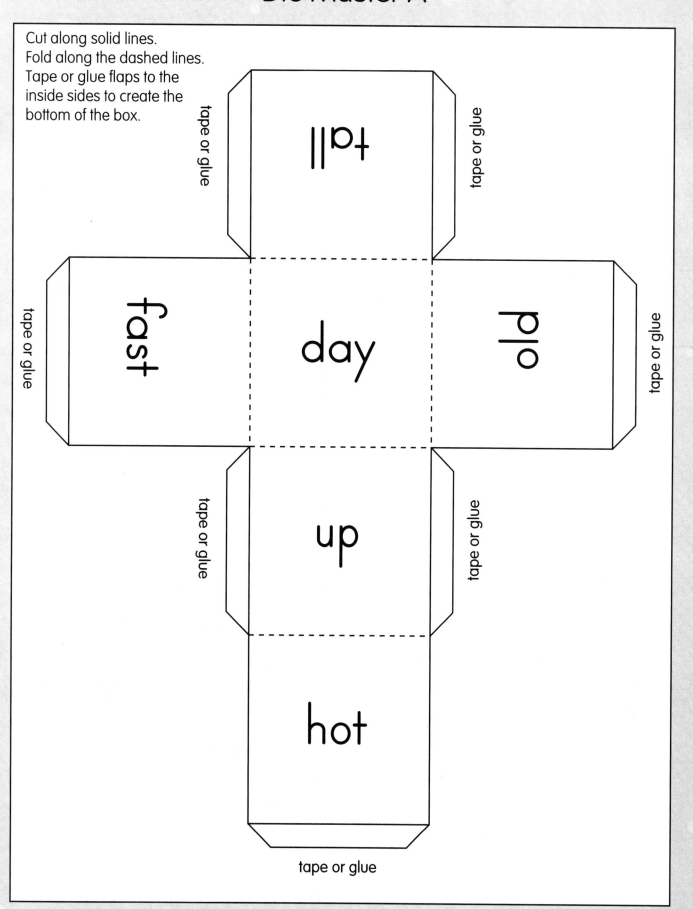

Die Master B

Cut along solid lines.
Fold along the dashed lines.
Tape or glue flaps to the inside sides to create the bottom of the box.

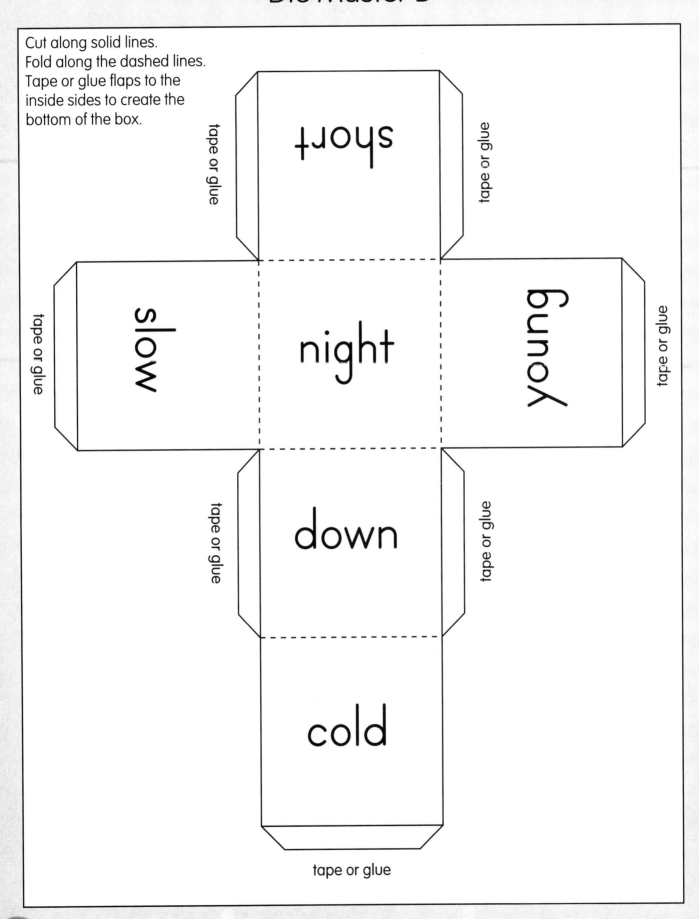

#50700   *Early Childhood Vocabulary Development Activities*

Blank Die Master

Cut along solid lines.
Fold along the dashed lines.
Tape or glue flaps to the inside sides to create the bottom of the box.

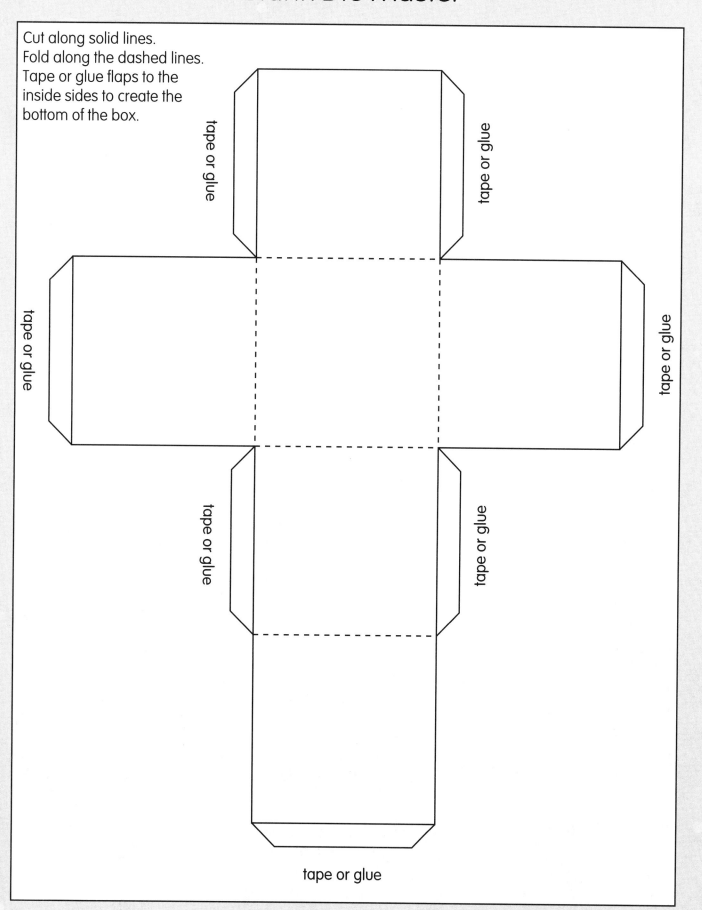

Size 'Em Up

Suggested Group Size:

Small group (2–6 students)

Activity Overview:

Students will put together puzzles that compare three objects and will describe those objects using appropriate vocabulary.

Materials:

- "Ice Cream Picture Cards" (page 68)
- "Puzzle Pieces" (pages 69–71)
- 3 pencils of different sizes
- 18 3" x 5" (8 cm x 13 cm) index cards
- one red and one blue marker
- a large envelope

Vocabulary Words:

big	small
huge	little
large	tiny

Activity Preparation

1. Photocopy "Ice Cream Picture Cards" and "Puzzle Pieces" onto cardstock paper and color as desired (or print color copies from the CD).
2. Cut out "Ice Cream Picture Cards."
3. Laminate the cards and puzzles for durability.
4. Cut out all of the puzzle pieces on the dotted lines.
5. Store all of the puzzle pieces together in a large envelope.
6. Write each of the vocabulary words on an index card using a blue marker.

Building Background

Show the students the three "Ice Cream Picture Cards." Ask them what the differences are among the three pictures. Explain to the students that we can use special words to describe the sizes of objects that we see every day. Tell them that they will be building puzzles today that will help them learn some of these special size words.

Activity Procedure

1. Find three pencils, each a different size. Hold up the largest of the three pencils. Show the students the index card with the word *small* written on it. Explain to the students that *small* is a word that we can use to describe this pencil. Place the card next to the pencil. Show the students the next pencil. Write the word in blue again on a second index card. Using a red marker, add the suffix *-er* to make the word *smaller,* and place the card next to the second pencil. Finally, show the students the smallest pencil. Write the word in blue again on a third index card. Using a red marker, add the suffix *-est* to make the word *smallest,* and place the card next to the pencil. Have the students read the cards with you.

2. Review the remaining vocabulary words with the students. Practice adding the *-er* and the *-est* suffixes to those words.

3. Gather the students around a table and spread out all of the puzzle pieces in the center of the table. Tell the students that there are six different puzzles on the table and that each puzzle has four pieces. Show the students how to find four pieces that go together to make a complete puzzle. Point out that the first piece in the puzzle has a word written on it, and each of the other three pieces has a picture. The students will first use the word to describe the first picture, then the word + *-er* to describe the second picture, and finally the word + *-est* to describe the last picture of the puzzle. When a student finds four pieces that go together to make a puzzle, he or she yells, "Size 'em up!" Everyone freezes and listens to the student use the appropriate vocabulary to describe the three pictures in the four-piece puzzle. Then the student returns the separated puzzle pieces back into the center of the table and the game continues. Challenge each student to try to put together as many of the puzzles as possible.

Adaptations

- Hold up one of the index cards with a root word on it. Challenge the students to work with a partner to find three objects in the room that they can compare using the root word and the appropriate suffixes.

- Have the students create a family picture, drawing the family members in a line from biggest to smallest.

Related Books

Bumble Bugs and Elephants by Margaret Wise Brown

Kidogo by Anik McGrory

Ice Cream Picture Cards

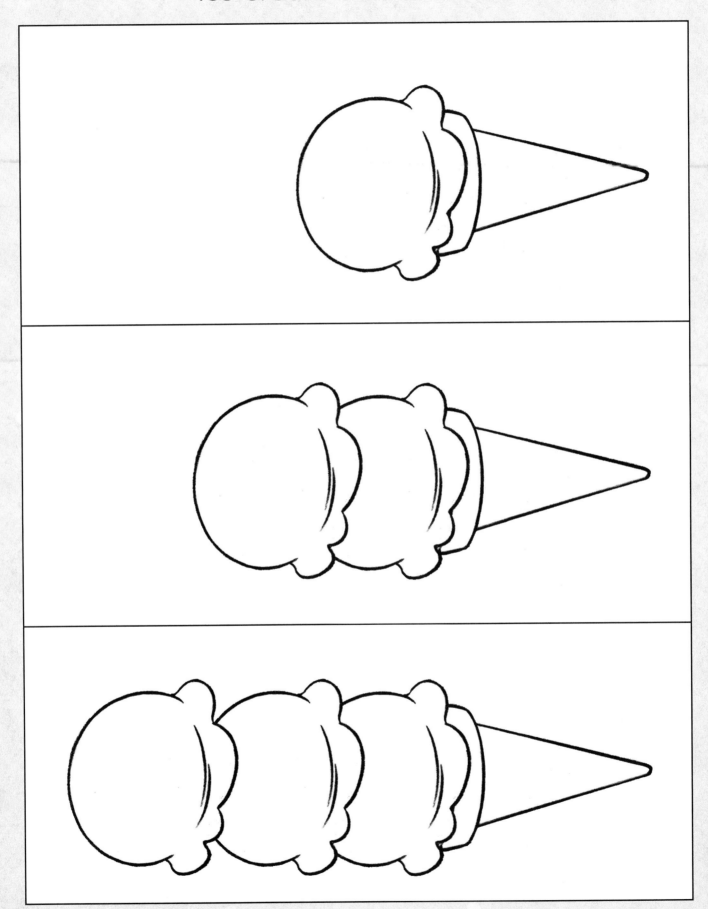

#50700   *Early Childhood Vocabulary Development Activities*

Puzzle Pieces

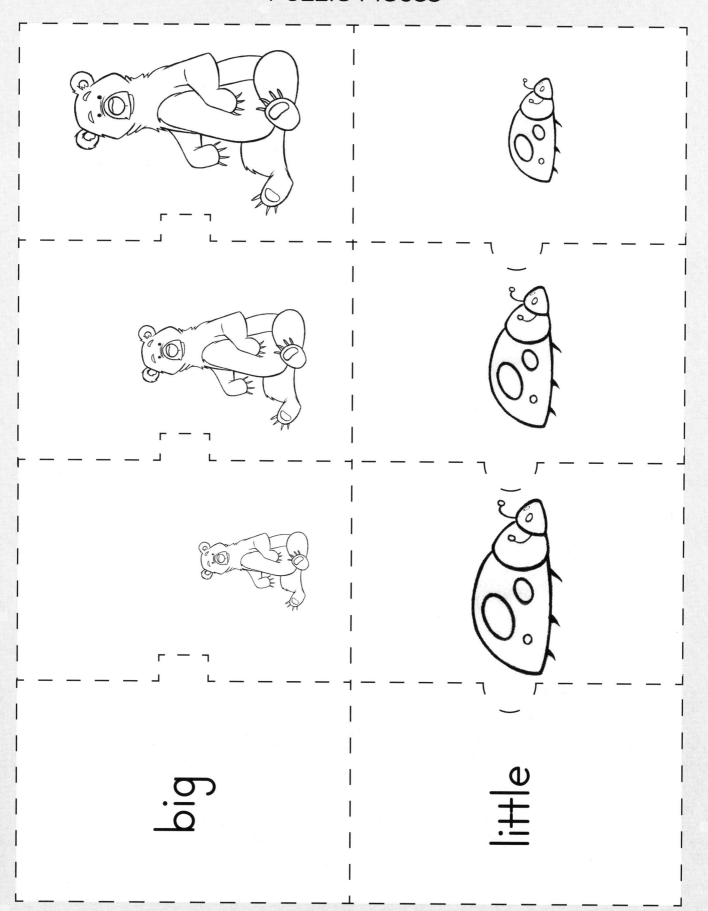

big

little

Puzzle Pieces *(cont.)*

large

small

#50700   *Early Childhood Vocabulary Development Activities*

Puzzle Pieces *(cont.)*

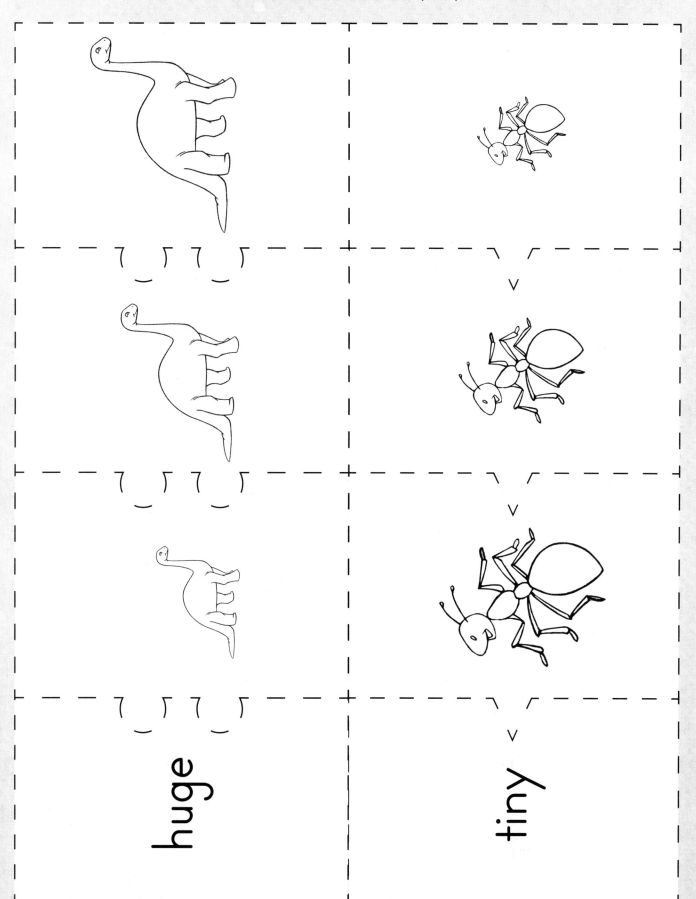

huge

tiny

Don't Bug Me!

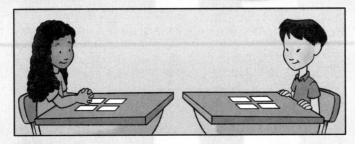

Skill:

Recognizing multi-meaning words

Suggested Group Size:

Small group (2–8)

Activity Overview:

Students will play a card game with a partner to demonstrate their understanding of selected multi-meaning words.

Materials:

- "Multi-Meaning Word Cards" (pages 74–75)
- green and yellow paper

Vocabulary Words:

bat	fly
bug	play
duck	trunk
fair	

Activity Preparation

1. Photocopy "Multi-Meaning Word Cards" onto cardstock paper (or print color copies from the CD). This set will be for teacher use.
2. Cut out the cards, and laminate them for durability.
3. Photocopy one set of "Multi-Meaning Word Cards" for each student to use. Copy half of the sets on yellow construction paper and the other half on green construction paper.

Building Background

Ask the students if they know what the word *bug* means. Explain to the students that sometimes a word means more than one thing. *Bug* can mean a kind of insect. It also can mean to bother or annoy someone. (There are several other meanings as well.) Tell the students that today they are going to learn about multi-meaning words by playing a game called "Don't Bug Me!"

Activity Procedure

1. Review the words from the teacher set of the "Multi-Meaning Word Cards." There are seven word cards and one *bug card*, which will indicate that the game is over. Show them each word card, read the word aloud, and have the students try to come up with at least two meanings for each card. Help them with any meanings that are unfamiliar.

2. Have each student sit at a desk with a partner. Pass out the "Multi-Meaning Word Cards" to each student. Be sure to give one partner a yellow copy and the other partner a green copy. Have the students cut out their cards. Model how to lay out the word cards and the bug card on the desk so that all students have two rows of four cards facedown in front of them and so that each student is facing his or her partner with the two sets of cards between them.

3. Explain the rules of the game. Model the procedure with a student partner before having the students do this alone. The player with the yellow set of cards (Player Y) begins the game. He or she points to one of the partner's green cards. The partner with the green set of cards (Player G) turns over that card and says, "Don't Bug Me!" if the bug card is not there. Player Y may either give one meaning for the word or use the word in a sentence. If Player Y is correct, then he or she gets to keep that card and sets it aside in a separate *win pile*. If Player Y is incorrect, then the card is returned facedown in the pile. The game continues with players taking turns with this procedure. The object of the game is to have the most cards in the win pile when the game is over. The game ends once one of the players finds the bug card in the other player's set. The player that finds the bug card first gets to add that card to his or her win pile.

Adaptations

- Have the students work with their partners to make a page for a class "Multi-Meaning Book." Using "Book Page" (page 175), have partners write an assigned multi-meaning word on the bottom of both halves of the paper. Then each partner can illustrate a different meaning for the word on his or her half of the page.

- Make copies of the "Blank Flip Card" master (page 176) for each pair of students. They can illustrate the two meanings for assigned multi-meaning words on the flip cards. (See the directions for making flip cards in the "Rolling for Opposites" activity on page 58.)

Related Books

How Much Can a Bare Bear Bear? by Brian Cleary

bat

bug

duck

fair

fly

play

trunk

Going on a Treasure Hunt

Skill:

Using appropriate location words

Suggested Group Size:

Whole class or small group

Activity Overview:

Students will use location words to find the treasure.

Materials:

- *We're Going on a Bear Hunt* by Michael Rosen (Clarion Books, 1989)
- "Treasure Hunt Direction Cards" (pages 78–79)
- "Treasure Chest" (page 80)
- "Treasure Chest Lid" (page 81)
- pocket chart
- blindfold
- small prizes for the treasure chest (e.g., stickers, chocolate coins, erasers, coupons, etc.)

Vocabulary Words:

around	onto
beneath	over
between	through
inside	under

Activity Preparation

1. Photocopy "Treasure Hunt Direction Cards" onto cardstock paper (or print color copies from the CD).
2. Cut out the word cards, and laminate them for durability.
3. Photocopy "Treasure Chest" and "Treasure Chest Lid" onto cardstock paper, and color as desired (or print color copies from the CD).
4. Assemble the treasure chest pattern and supply small prizes on top of it.

Building Background

Read *We're Going on a Bear Hunt* to the students. Explain to the students that the author used special words in the story to describe how they got to their destination on their hunt for the bear. Tell the students that they will be going on another kind of hunt. Since there are no bears at school, the students will be going on a "treasure hunt" instead.

Activity Procedure

1. Use the "Treasure Hunt Direction Cards" to review the vocabulary with the students. Post the words or put them in a pocket chart for the students to refer to during the activity.

2. Select a student to demonstrate his or her understanding of the words by giving directions on how to get from one side of the room to the other. For example, you might tell the student to walk *between* the chairs and *around* the desk, crawl *under* the table, and walk *around* the ball box to get to the door.

3. Show the students the "treasure chest." Explain to the students that the treasure chest will be hidden somewhere in the room while one of the students is blindfolded. Remove the blindfold from the selected student once the treasure is hidden. That student will be the "treasure hunter." After hiding the treasure chest, select another student to give directions to the treasure hunter, using some of the vocabulary words from the pocket chart that will lead him or her to the treasure chest. Once the chest has been found, the treasure hunter and the student that gave the directions may each take a "treasure" from the chest. Continue with the game until all the students have had a turn.

Adaptations

- Have the students take turns giving you directions on how to get from the door to your desk.

- Have the students create a class story. The students can pretend they are real treasure hunters who have found a treasure. Have them dictate a story to you telling of their adventure as you write the words on chart paper. The students should use as many of the words from the "Treasure Hunt Direction Cards" as possible.

- Make enough treasure chests and lids for each student or each pair of students to find their own treasures.

Related Books

Where Does the Trail Lead? by Burton Albert
All About Where by Tana Hoban

around	beneath
between	inside

 #50700 *Early Childhood Vocabulary Development Activities*

onto	over
through	under

Treasure Chest

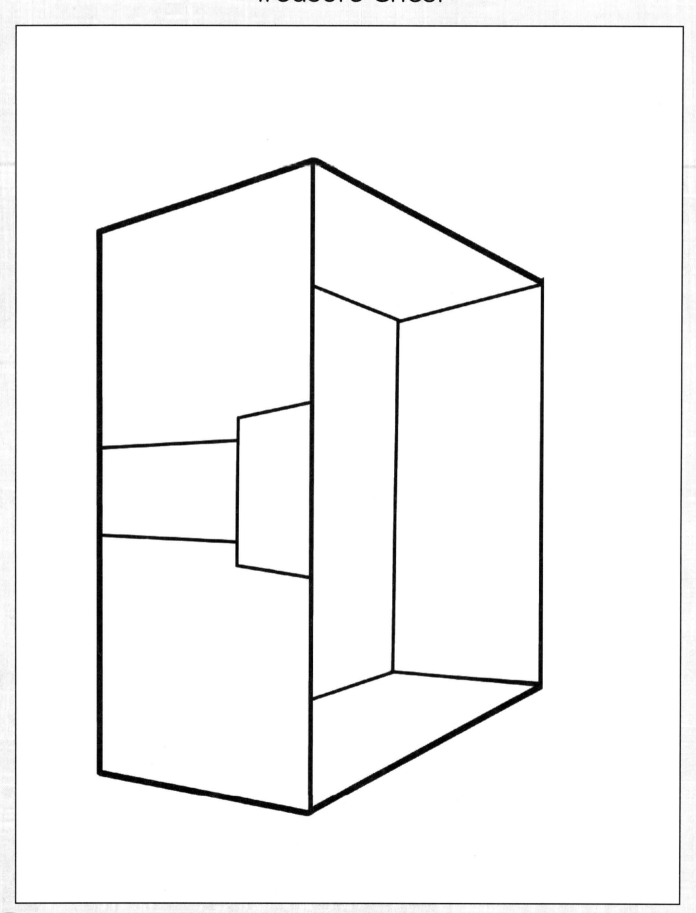

#50700   *Early Childhood Vocabulary Development Activities*

Treasure Chest Lid

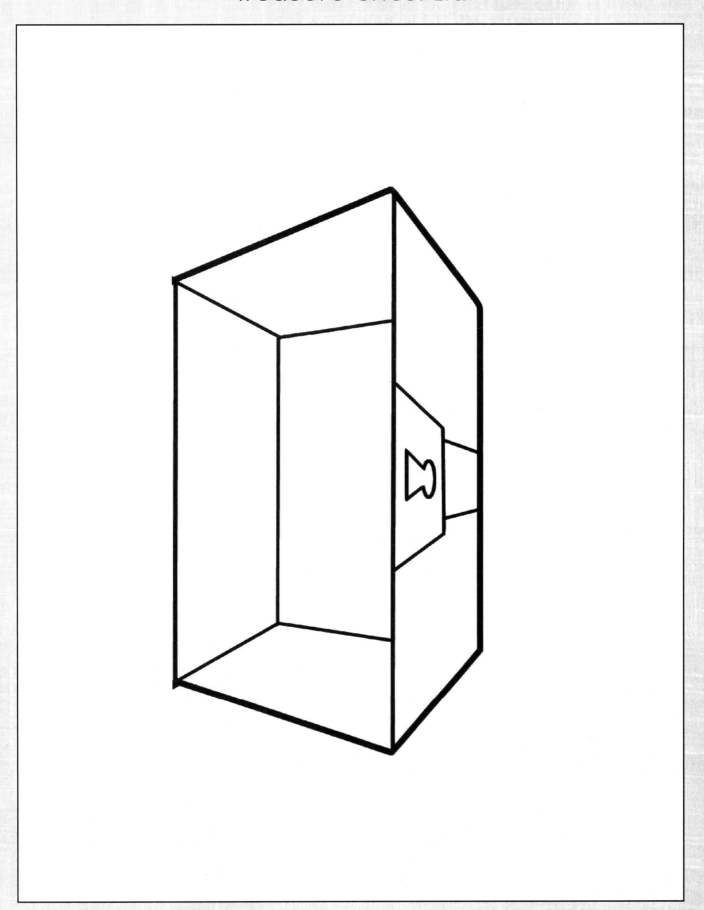

Don't Spill the Beans

Skill:

Recognizing idioms and their meanings

Suggested Group Size:

Small group (4–6 students)

Activity Overview:

Students will earn beans for their teams by selecting correct definitions for common idioms.

Materials:

- "Common Idioms and Their Definitions" (page 84)
- "Idiom Picture Cards–Set A" (pages 85–87)
- a bell or other object that the students may use to indicate when they have an answer
- small container of beans

Idioms:

Don't spill the beans.

He's under the weather.

I've got butterflies in my stomach.

She got up on the wrong side of the bed.

I get a kick out of that!

There are ants in my pants!

Activity Preparation

1. Photocopy "Idiom Picture Cards–Set A" onto cardstock paper, and color as desired (or make color copies from the CD).
2. Cut out "Idiom Picture Cards–Set A", and laminate for durability.
3. Make a photocopy of "Common Idioms and Their Definitions" page for reference during the activity.

Building Background

Show the students one of the beans, and ask them if they have ever heard the saying *"Don't spill the beans!"* Demonstrate the literal definition by spilling some beans from the container. Explain to the students that some sayings like "Don't spill the beans!" actually have more than one meaning. Tell the students about a time when you or someone you know *spilled the beans* or told someone something that should have been kept secret. Then use the idiom in a sentence. Allow time for the students to share a time when they may have "spilled the beans."

Activity Procedure

1. Tell the students that they are going to play a game called "Don't Spill the Beans!" Divide the group in half. One team will be Team A, and the other will be Team B. The object of the game is to be the team with the most beans.

2. Play one practice round first to model the procedure. Have one student from each team come up to the front by you. The two students should face each other with the bell between them and with their hands behind their backs. Show the students the first "Idiom Picture Card," and read the idiom that is written on the card. Give the students the chance to ring the bell, and tell you the definition of the idiom. Explain to the students that if neither student knows the definition, you will tell them two simple definitions for the idiom, only one of which is correct. Refer to "Common Idioms and Their Definitions" for the real definitions. After you have said the two definitions, the two students attempt to be the first to ring the bell. Say to the rest of the class, "Don't spill the beans!" which means they cannot help their teammates by giving them the answer, or the other team will earn a bean. The student who rings the bell first answers by saying the definition that he or she thinks is correct. If the answer is correct, award that team a bean.

3. The game continues in this manner until all of the picture cards have been played.

Adaptations

- Use "Idiom Picture Cards–Set B" (pages 88–90) for another round of "Don't Spill the Beans!"

- Have the students work with partners to make a "Class Idiom Book." Using the "Idiom Book Page" (page 91), have the students illustrate the meaning of assigned idioms. Collect the pages and bind them to make the book.

- Select one of the "Idiom Picture Cards" to be the idiom of the week. Every time a student shares a personal example that uses the idiom, ring the game bell and announce it to the class. Have the student share the example with the other students.

- The Internet is a wonderful resource for lists, definitions, and examples of many more idioms.

Related Books

Monkey Business by Wallace Edwards
Super Silly Sayings That Are Over Your Head: A Children's Illustrated Book of Idioms by Catherine Snodgrass

Common Idioms and Their Definitions

Set A

Don't spill the beans.................... To not tell a secret

He's under the weather............... Feeling ill

I've got butterflies in my stomach........ Feeling nervous or fearful

He got up on the wrong side of the bed... Being in a bad mood

I get a kick out of that!................. Thinking something is funny

There are ants in my pants!............ Feeling restless or impatient

Set B

That's a piece of cake! .... Simple to do

Drop me a line....................... To call or write someone

Give him a hand...................... 1. To applaud someone
2. To help someone

That costs an arm and a leg!.......... Costing a lot of money

I'm feeling down in the dumps......... Feeling sad or depressed

It's raining cats and dogs!............. Raining very hard

 #50700   *Early Childhood Vocabulary Development Activities*

Don't spill the beans.

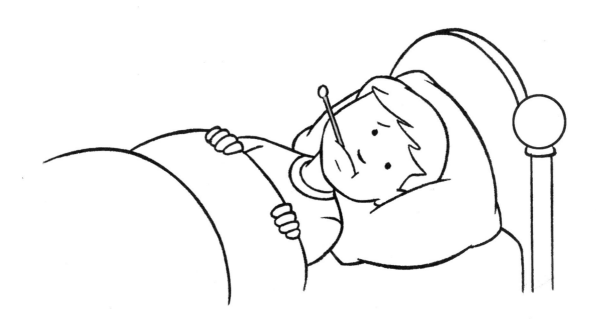

He's under the weather.

I've got butterflies in my stomach.

He got up on the wrong side of the bed.

I get a kick out of that!

There are ants in my pants!

That's a piece of cake!

Drop me a line.

#50700   *Early Childhood Vocabulary Development Activities*

Give him a hand.

That costs an arm and a leg!

I'm feeling down in the dumps.

It's raining cats and dogs!

Idiom Book Page

Name: _____

_____

- -

_____

- -

_____

- -

_____

Home Sweet Home

Skill:

Recognizing names of animal homes

Suggested Group Size:

Whole class or small group

Activity Overview:

Students will make spinners to learn the types of homes in which different animals live.

Materials:

- "Animal Home Spinners" (pages 94–97)
- one straw or unsharpened pencil for each student
- glue
- transparent tape

Vocabulary Words:

burrow	hive
cave	nest
den	tree
coop	hill

Activity Preparation

1. Photocopy one set of "Animal Home Spinners" onto cardstock paper to make a sample, and color as desired (or make color copies from the CD).
2. Cut out "Animal Home Spinners," and laminate for durability.
3. Make all of the spinners except one. Fold each in half on the dotted line. Tape a pencil or straw to the inside. Glue the two sides closed, leaving the bottom open. Save the last spinner to model how to put one together during the activity.
4. Make enough photocopies of the "Animal Home Spinners" for each student to make one. Copy on 9" x 12" (23 cm x 30 cm) white construction paper.

Building Background

Ask the students if they have any pets. Have them discuss the kinds of homes their pets live in (e.g., cage, fishbowl, doghouse). Explain to the students that animals in the wild have to find their own homes, and today they will be learning the names of some of those special homes.

Activity Procedure

1. Model how to make one of the "Animal Home Spinners" using one of the samples. Cut out one and fold it in half on the dotted line. Tape a pencil or straw to the inside. Glue the two sides closed, leaving the bottom open. Insert a straw or pencil into the bottom opening of the spinner. Demonstrate how to hold the pencil between your two hands, and spin it by rubbing your hands back and forth. Ask the students to watch closely as you spin it. The animal on the front of the spinner will appear to be inside the home on the back of the spinner.

2. Pass out one of the "Animal Home Spinners" to each student and have each student make his or her own. Have the students practice spinning their spinners. Provide an opportunity for the students to share spinners so that everyone gets an opportunity to see each of the eight animal homes.

3. Call out an animal name that appears on one of the sample spinners. Ask the students who have that animal to stand and tell you the name of that animal's home, or read it together. Have them spin the spinner once again, and then sit down. Repeat with the remaining spinners.

Adaptations

- Quiz the students on how well they know the names of the animal homes. Give them three clues about each home, including the name of an animal that might live there, and have them guess which home it might be.

Related Books

A House Is a House for Me by Mary Ann Hoberman

Animal Home Spinners

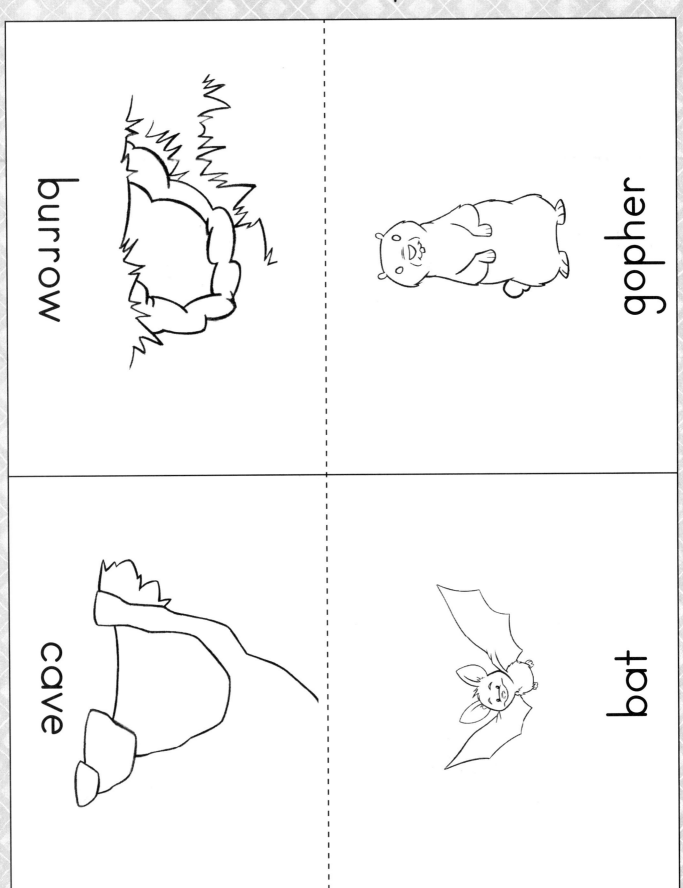

burrow

gopher

cave

bat

#50700   *Early Childhood Vocabulary Development Activities*

hive

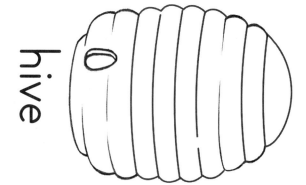

bee

nest

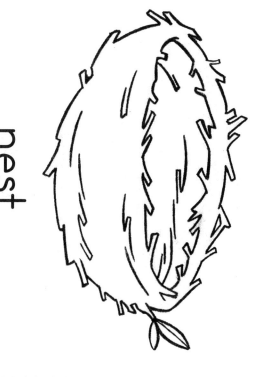

bird

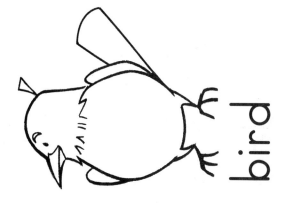

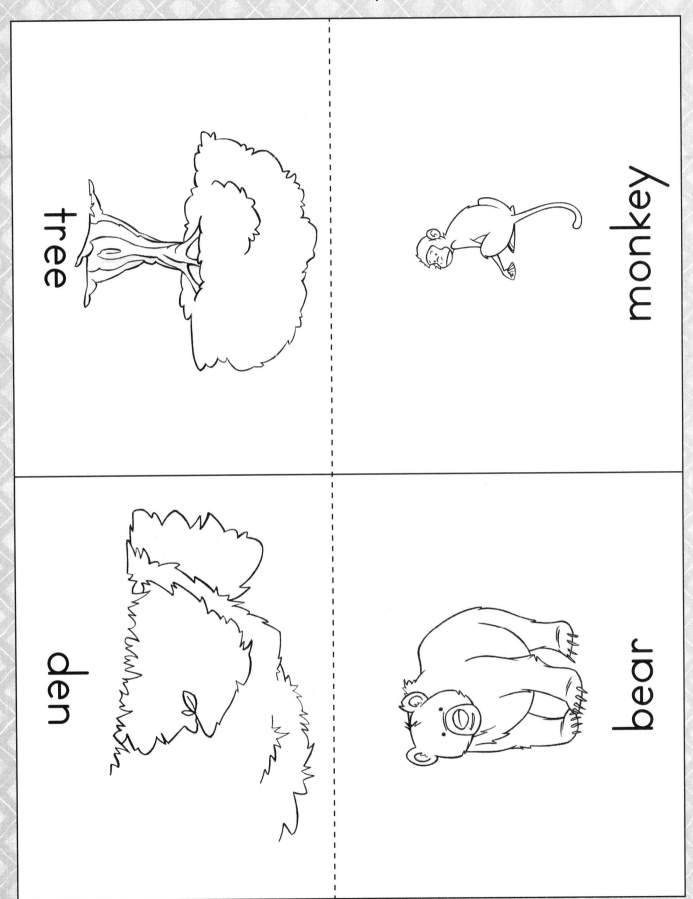

tree

monkey

den

bear

#50700   *Early Childhood Vocabulary Development Activities*

Animal Home Spinners (cont.)

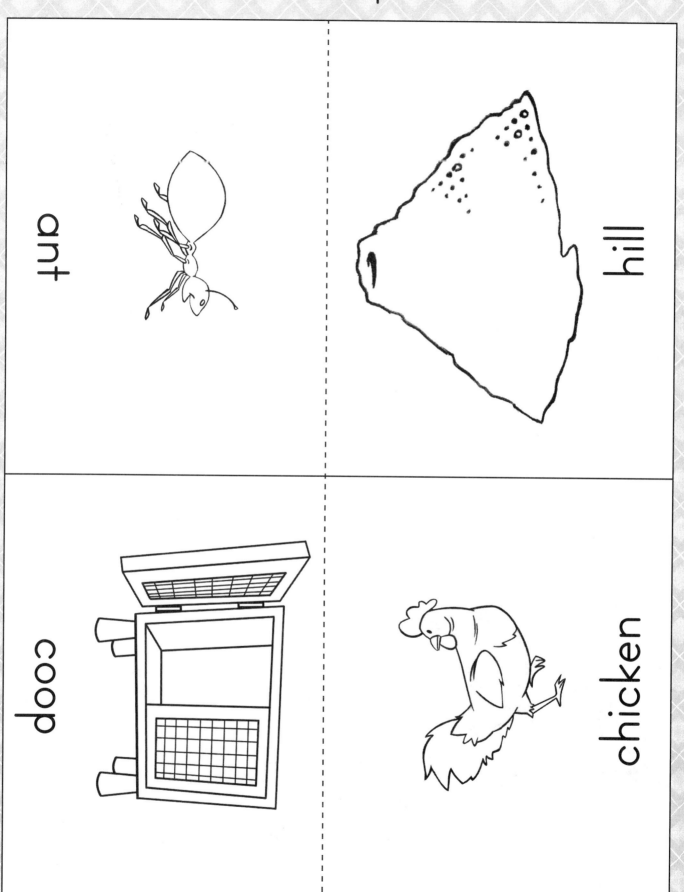

ant

hill

coop

chicken

Maggie's First Day

Suggested Group Size:

Whole class

Activity Overview:

Students will participate in a read-aloud activity by acting out feelings portrayed by characters in a story.

Materials:

- "Feeling Faces" (pages 100–102)
- "Faces, Bodies, and Sounds" (page 102)
- "Maggie's First Day" (page 103)

Vocabulary Words:

angry	sad
excited	worried
proud	

Activity Preparation

1. Photocopy "Feeling Faces" onto cardstock paper, and color as desired (or print color copies from the CD).
2. Cut apart the "Feeling Faces," and laminate for durability.

Building Background

Tell the students about your recollections of your first day of school and all the feelings you had that day. Ask the students to share their feelings about their first day of school. Show the students the "Feeling Faces," and let them know that today they will be learning some words that describe how people feel.

Activity Procedure

1. Point out the *angry* "Feeling Faces" card. Ask the students to note the eyes and the mouth on the face. Ask the students to mimic the expression on the card after you model for them. Then model the body language that goes with this feeling, perhaps placing the fists on the hips. Finally, model the sound "Grrr!" that the students will associate with this feeling. Have the students practice doing the facial expression, the body language, and the sound that goes with *angry*.

2. Repeat this procedure with the remaining "Feeling Faces" cards, teaching the students the facial expression, the body language, and the sound for each card. Refer to the "Faces, Bodies, and Sounds" page for ideas.

3. Divide the students into five groups. Pass out one of the "Feeling Faces" to each group. Tell the students that you will be reading a story to the class called *Maggie's First Day*. Each time a group hears its feeling word in the story, they should make the facial expression, body language gesture, and the sound for that feeling. As you read the story out loud, pause after reading each feeling word to give the students time to perform the feeling word.

Adaptations

- Have a volunteer select a feeling word without telling the class which word was selected. Have the student act out the word, and have the students guess which feeling is being performed.

- Select books to share with the class that have pictures of characters whose facial expressions show examples of feeling words described in the lesson. Characters found in fairy tales and folktales are perfect for this.

Related Books

What Makes Me Happy? by Catherine Anholt and Laurence Anholt
Walter Was Worried by Laura Vaccaro Seeger

angry

excited

proud

sad

scared

Faces, Bodies, and Sounds

Feeling	Facial Expression	Body Language	Sound
angry	Eyebrows pointed down in the middle, mouth turned down	Hands on hips	*Grrr!*
excited	Eyes wide open, wide smile	Hands in the air	*Yippee*
proud	Wide smile	Standing tall, shoulders back, arms to the sides	*Yeah!*
sad	Arms wrapped around self	Lower lip stuck out, eyes looking down	*Boo, hoo!*
scared	Eyes wide	Biting fingernails, legs shaking	*Yikes!*

Maggie's First Day

Tomorrow would be the first day of school and Maggie was EXCITED. She had already picked out the outfit she would wear and was PROUD of her choice. She ran around the house all day long telling everyone in her family just how EXCITED she was. Maggie went to bed that evening looking forward to the next day.

When Maggie awoke, her stomach was feeling a little strange. She was no longer looking forward to going to school. Maggie was SCARED. The thought of riding in the bus made her SCARED. The idea of meeting her teacher and her classmates made her SCARED. Spending all day in a new classroom made her SCARED. And thinking about not seeing her parents all day made her SAD.

Maggie's parents found Maggie still in bed. They told Maggie how PROUD they were of her and how EXCITED they would be to hear all about her first day of school when she arrived back home. Soon they realized that Maggie wasn't feeling so EXCITED. She just looked a little SAD. Maggie's big brother came in just then. He told Maggie that she was just SCARED about going to school. This made Maggie ANGRY. She didn't want her brother to think she was SCARED. She jumped out of bed and stomped around the room looking for her clothing and showing her big brother just how ANGRY she was at him. In no time at all, Maggie was dressed and ready to go.

When Maggie got home that afternoon, she was all smiles. Maggie was PROUD of herself for being so brave after having felt so SAD and SCARED inside this morning. She was still a little ANGRY at her brother, but she was EXCITED to tell him what a brave girl she had been. She knew her family would be very PROUD of her indeed.

Handshakes

Skill:
Recognizing common compound words

Suggested Group Size:
Small group
(4 pairs of students)

Activity Overview:
Students will identify two words that create a compound word when put together.

Materials:
- "Handshake Cards" (page 106)
- "Compound Word Picture Cards–Set A" (page 107)
- "Compound Word Picture Cards–Set B" (page 108)

Vocabulary Words:
handshake
cupcake
football
houseboat
ladybug

Activity Preparation

1. Photocopy "Compound Word Picture Cards–Set A" onto cardstock paper, and color as desired (or print color copies from the CD). With a marker, write the letter **A** on the back of each card.
2. Photocopy "Compound Word Picture Cards–Set B" onto cardstock paper, and color as desired (or print color copies from the CD). With a marker, write the letter **B** on the back of each card.
3. Cut out the cards, and laminate them for durability.
4. Photocopy "Handshake Cards" onto cardstock paper, and color as desired (or print color copies from the CD).
5. Cut out "Handshake Cards," and glue both cards together back-to-back. Laminate for durability.

Building Background

Show the students the side of the "Handshake Cards" that has the picture of the *hand* + the picture of the *shake*. Explain that some words in the English language called *compound words* are made up of two separate words that are put together. Sometimes the students can guess what a compound word means if they know the meanings of the two words that make up the compound word. Show the students the backside of the "Handshake Cards." Discuss the words *hand* and *shake* and how they can be used to figure out the meaning of *handshake*.

Activity Procedure

1. Divide the students into two groups, with four students in each group. Have each group line up shoulder to shoulder facing a person from the other group. Pass out one of the "Compound Word Picture Cards–Set A" to each student in one group and one of the "Compound Word Picture Cards–Set B" to each student in the other group. Have the students hold their cards in front of them so that the other team can see their pictures.

2. Tell the students that they are going to play a game called "Handshakes." The object of the game is for each person in group *A* to find a person in group *B* who has a picture that makes a compound word when matched with theirs. The first student in the *A* group looks at his or her own card, looks for any student in the *B* group who has a picture that would create a compound word, and walks up to shake that person's hand. Together they show the class their pictures and tell everyone what the compound word is. If their word is correct, they may sit down together. If their word is not correct, both students return to their spots. You may want to give the *A* group student another try, and help by reading all of the possible compound words that can be made using his or her card.

3. Continue with this procedure until each student has been correctly paired with a student from the other team.

Adaptations

- Use the "Compound Word Picture Cards–Set C" (page 109) and the "Compound Word Picture Cards–Set D" (page 110) to play another round of "Handshakes" or to play with a larger group of students.

- Make enough copies of the "Handshakes Book Page" (page 111) for each pair of students to share. After finding a partner and shaking his or her hand, each pair may return to their seats with their book page to illustrate their compound word. Have each student write his or her picture word in one of the hands at the bottom of the page and the compound word on the line indicated. Bind all of the pages together to create a class book.

Related Books

All Aboard Overnight: A Book of Compound Words by Betsy Maestro and Giulio Maestro

Handshake Cards

hand + shake

handshake

#50700 *Early Childhood Vocabulary Development Activities* © *Shell Education*

Compound Word Picture Cards-Set A

cup

foot

house

lady

Compound Word Picture Cards-Set B

cake

ball

boat

bug

#50700   *Early Childhood Vocabulary Development Activities*

Compound Word Picture Cards-Set C

mail

paint

rain

star

Compound Word Picture Cards-Set D

box

brush

coat

fish

Handshakes Book Page

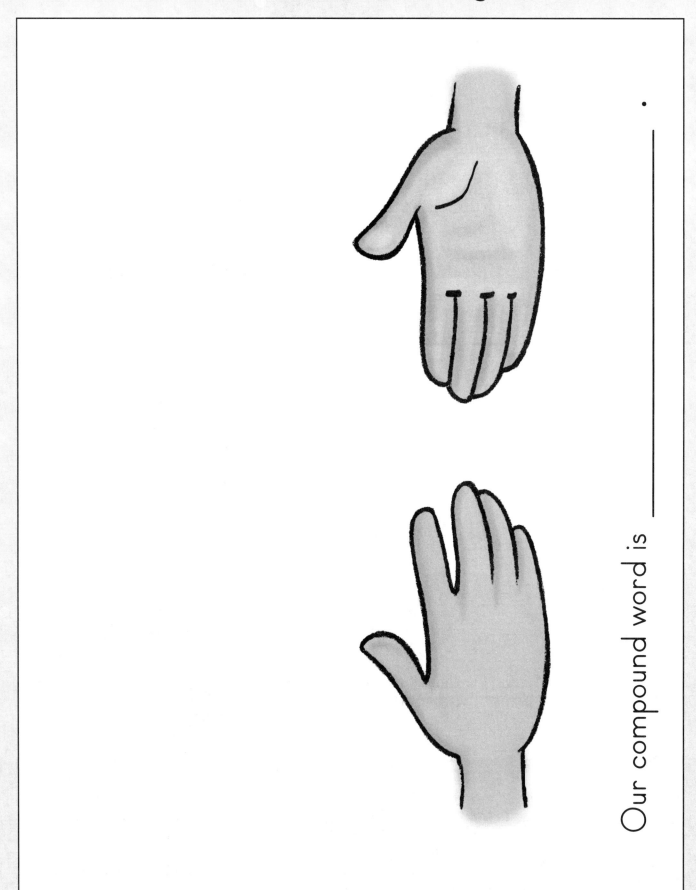

Our compound word is _____ .

Compound Clues

Activity Preparation

Skill:

Recognizing compound words

Suggested Group Size:

Small group (4–8 students)

Activity Overview:

Students will use picture clues to figure out compound words with nonpredictable meanings.

Materials:

- "Picture Clues" (pages 114–115)
- "Compound Word Cards" (pages 116–117)
- "Handshake Cards" (See "Handshakes" lesson, page 106)
- pocket chart

Vocabulary Words:

bedspread	horsefly
butterfly	pigtail
doughnut	rainbow
greenhouse	wishbone

1. Photocopy "Picture Clues," "Compound Word Cards," and the "Handshake Cards" onto cardstock paper, and color as desired (or print colored copies from the CD).

2. Laminate "Picture Clues," "Compound Word Cards," and the "Handshake Cards" for durability, and cut them out.

3. Write the letter **A** on the back of the *bedspread* "Picture Clues" card. Write the letter **B** on the back of the *butterfly* "Picture Clues" card. Continue writing a letter on the back of each remaining "Picture Clues" card using the letters **C** through **F**.

4. Place the "Compound Word Cards" facedown in the pocket chart in two rows with four cards in each row.

5. Place the "Picture Clues" cards on top of their corresponding "Compound Word Cards" so that the letter on the back of each card can be seen.

6. Glue together the two "Handshake Cards" back-to-back.

Building Background

Show the students the side of the "Handshake Cards" that has the picture of the hand + the picture of the shaking or shivering person. Explain that some words in the English language called compound words are made up of two separate words that are put together. Sometimes the students can guess what a compound word means if they know the meanings of the two words that make up the compound word. Show the students the backside of the "Handshake Cards." Discuss the words *hand* and *shake* and how they can be used to figure out the meaning of *handshake*. Tell the students that today, however, they will be learning some compound words whose meanings are not so easy to figure out based on the two words that make up each of the compound words.

Activity Procedure

1. Select a volunteer to choose one of the letters that has been written on the "Picture Clues" cards in the pocket chart. Turn over the chosen letter card so that the students can see the picture clue. Read aloud the definition at the bottom of the card. Have the students use the definition and the picture clues to guess what compound word appears on the corresponding "Compound Word Card." Once the word is guessed correctly, turn over the "Compound Word Card" so the students can see the picture and the compound word written on the bottom of the card.

2. Continue with this procedure until all the "Picture Clues" have been correctly guessed.

Adaptations

- Have the students dictate sentences to you using the compound words from the lesson. Write each sentence on a blank sheet of paper, and have volunteers illustrate each page.

- Create a class poster for the students to write compound words that they find while reading.

Related Books

Flying Butter by Patricia Trattles

Once There Was a Bull...(Frog) by Rick Walton

Picture Clues

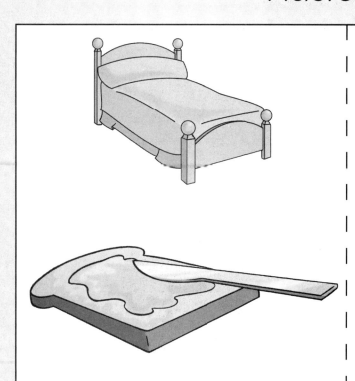
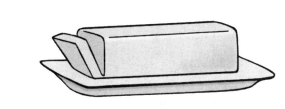

A type of covering for a bed | An insect with beautiful wings

A small ring-shaped cake that is eaten for breakfast | A special glass building used for growing plants

#50700   Early Childhood Vocabulary Development Activities

Braided hair gathered with a band or clip

A colorful object that can sometimes be seen in the sky after it rains

A horse-shoe shaped bone found in chickens

A type of large flying insect

Compound Word Cards

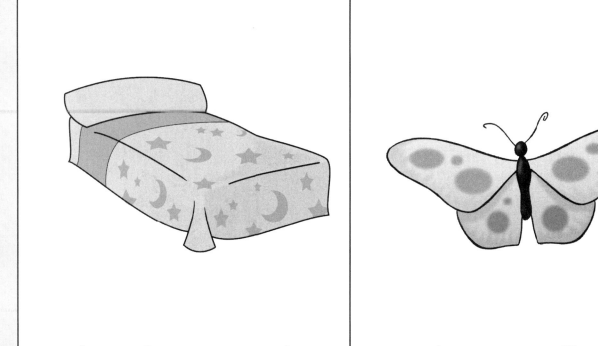

bedspread

butterfly

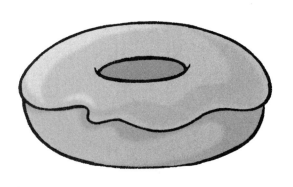

doughnut

greenhouse

#50700   Early Childhood Vocabulary Development Activities

Compound Word Cards (cont.)

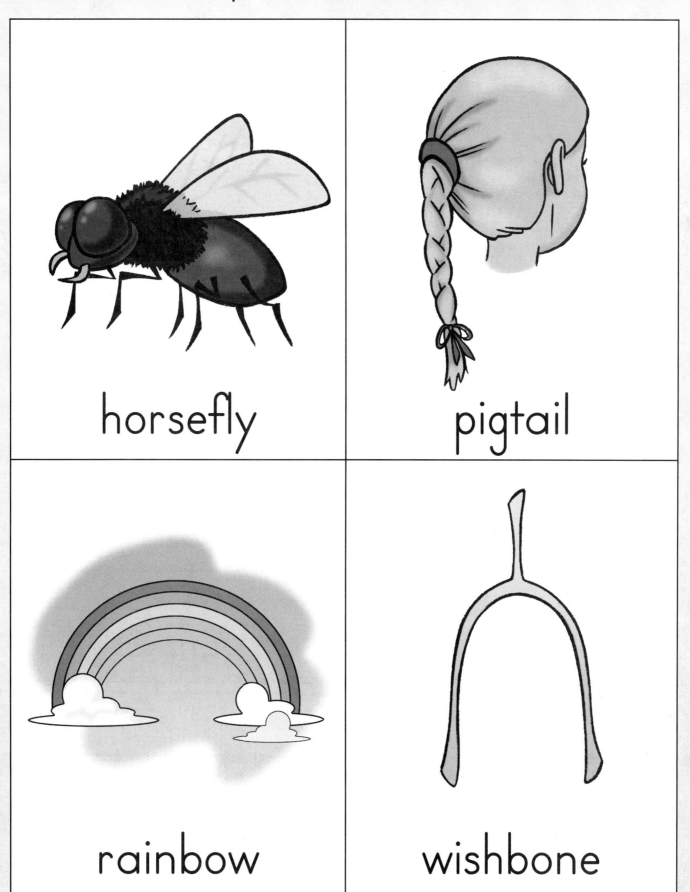

horsefly

pigtail

rainbow

wishbone

School Supplies

Skill:

Recognizing names for common school supplies and classroom items

Suggested Group Size:

Small group of 9 students

Activity Overview:

Students will play a listening game in which they must identify names of common school supplies and classroom items.

Materials:

- "School Supply Cards" (pages 120–121)
- "I Have...Who Has Cards" (page 122)
- sample objects from the vocabulary list
- eight 3" x 5" (8 cm x 13 cm) index cards
- pocket chart

Vocabulary Words:

book	eraser
chair	paint
crayons	paper
desk	pencil

Activity Preparation

1. Photocopy "School Supply Cards" and "I Have...Who Has Cards" on cardstock paper, and color as desired (or print color copies from the CD).
2. Cut out the cards, and laminate for durability.
3. Place the "School Supply Cards" in the pocket chart.

Building Background

Explain to the students that today they will be focusing on names for objects in the classroom. Show the students one of the sample objects. Have the students state the name of the object if they know it. Have a volunteer come up to the pocket chart, and find the card that names the object you are holding. Have the student show the word to the class, and then tell what the object is used for. Continue with the remaining objects.

#50700   *Early Childhood Vocabulary Development Activities*

Activity Procedure

1. Tell the students that they will be playing a listening game called "I Have...Who Has." Shuffle the cards, and pass one out to each student. Any extra cards need to be distributed to the students who will not have difficulty focusing on two cards at once.

2. Have the students look at the picture at the top of their cards. The person with the "Go!" card goes first by reading aloud the card that says, "Who has the book?" The rest of the students need to look to see if the picture of the book appears at the top of their cards. The student who has the card reads his or her own card aloud to the class by saying, "I have the book. Who has the chair?" The game continues in this manner until the student with the "Stop!" sign at the bottom of the card reads his or her card.

Adaptations

- Use the blank set of "I Have...Who Has Cards" (page 123) to make another set of school supply cards using words instead of pictures.
- Use the blank set of "I Have...Who Has Cards" (page 123) to make games for other vocabulary topics.

Related Books

I Spy School Days by Jean Marzollo

School Supplies: A Book of Poems by Lee Bennette Hopkins

School Supplies Cards–Set A

book

chair

crayons

desk

#50700   *Early Childhood Vocabulary Development Activities*

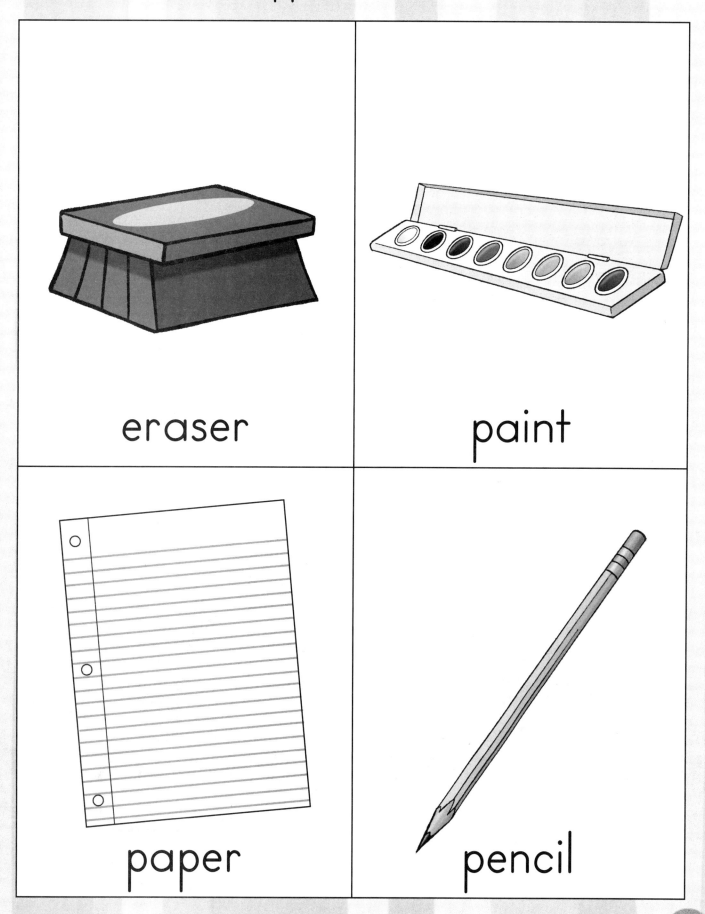

eraser

paint

paper

pencil

I Have... Who Has Cards

Who has the

I have the

Who has the

I have the

Who has the

I have the

Who has the

I have the

Who has the

I have the

Who has the

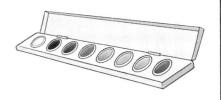

I have the

Who has the

I have the

Who has the

I have the

#50700   Early Childhood Vocabulary Development Activities

Blank I Have... Who Has Cards

GO! Who has the	I have the Who has the	I have the Who has the
I have the Who has the	I have the Who has the	I have the Who has the
I have the Who has the	I have the Who has the	I have the **STOP!**

School Bell

Skill:

Recognizing names for school workers and the jobs they perform

Suggested Group Size:

Whole class

Activity Overview:

Students will play a card game asking them to state the names of school workers and the jobs they perform.

Materials:

- "School Bell Cards" (pages 126–127)
- pocket chart
- bell (optional)

Vocabulary Words:

custodian	principal
librarian	secretary
lunch helper	teacher
nurse	school bell

Activity Preparation

1. Photocopy "School Bell Cards" onto cardstock paper, and color as desired (or print color copies from the CD). Make enough copies for each player to have one card (e.g., for 20 students, you will need 20 cards). Extra cards may be saved for future use. Use only one bell card during the game.

2. Cut out the cards, and laminate them for durability.

Building Background

Ask the students to name as many people as they can think of in one minute who work at their school. Show the students the "School Bell Cards," placing them inside the pocket chart one at a time. Explain to them that today they will be learning about the people on these cards and the jobs that they do.

Activity Procedure

1. Review the cards with the students. Discuss with the students the types of responsibilities each school worker has. Show them the card with the school bell last. Tell them that today they will be playing a game called "School Bell" to help them learn about these important people.

2. Have the students sit in a circle on the floor. Collect all of the "School Bell Cards," including the bell card, and shuffle them. Scatter the cards on the floor facedown in the center of the circle. Place the real bell in the center as well if one is available.

3. Have a student begin the game by selecting a card. The student then shows the card to the class, states the name of the school worker, and says one job that the school worker performs. The card is then left on the floor in front of the student for everyone to see for the duration of the game.

4. Continue going around the circle with each student taking a turn with this procedure until someone selects the bell card. The student who selects that card must ring the real bell (or yell "School Bell"), and then immediately go around the circle naming the school workers that appear on each card previously selected by his or her classmates.

5. Collect all the cards, reshuffle, and play another round beginning with the student in the circle whose turn would have been next.

Adaptations

- Invite each school worker to visit the class before playing the game to discuss his or her job.
- Have the students take turns sitting in a seat in front of the class. Each student should pretend to be one of the school workers, and give the class two clues to help them guess which worker he or she is pretending to be.

Related Books

Community Helpers: School Secretaries by Mary Firestone

That's Our Nurse! by Ann Morris

That's Our Principal! by Ann Morris

School Bell Cards

custodian

librarian

lunch helper

nurse

#50700   Early Childhood Vocabulary Development Activities

principal

secretary

teacher

school bell

Build a Weather Bear

Skill:

Understanding weather terms

Suggested Group Size:

Whole class

Activity Overview:

Students will work together in teams to outfit a bear based on an assigned type of weather.

Materials:

- "Weather Bear Picture Cards" (pages 130–131)
- "Weather Wheel" (page 132)
- "Weather Bear" (page 133)
- "Weather Items" (pages 134–135)
- paper clip
- pencil

Vocabulary Words:

rainy
snowy
sunny
windy

Activity Preparation

1. Photocopy "Weather Bear Picture Cards" and "Weather Wheel" onto cardstock paper, and color as desired (or print color copies from the CD).

2. Cut out all of the photocopied items, and laminate for durability.

3. Make two photocopies of "Weather Bear" on white copy paper and cut in half to make four bears. Write one of the following vocabulary words on the top of each page: *rainy, snowy, sunny, windy*.

4. Make one photocopy of "Weather Items" on white copy paper, and cut out the cards.

5. Place each of the "Weather Bear Picture Cards" in a row at the top of the pocket chart.

Building Background

Take the students on a "weather walk" outside. Have them look at the sky and describe what they see. Have them look at the leaves on the trees or a flag, and ask the students to describe the movement of these objects. Ask them to tell you whether they think it is hot, warm, or cold outside. Explain to the students that all of the things they looked for during their walk have to do with the weather. Tell the students that today they will be learning about four different kinds of weather.

#50700   *Early Childhood Vocabulary Development Activities*

Activity Procedure

1. Show the students each "Weather Bear Picture Card" in the pocket chart, read the title, and have them describe what they see in the pictures. Have them focus on the clothing each bear is wearing and the activity each bear is participating in. Then place each "Weather Items" card in a column below its corresponding "Weather Bear Picture Card," and discuss each item as you go.

2. Show the students the "Weather Wheel," and demonstrate how to use the spinner by placing the point of the pencil through one end of the paper clip and onto the center of the wheel. Then spin the paper clip by flicking the loose end with your finger. Placing the "Weather Wheel" on a flat surface works best.

3. Tell the students that they will be playing a team game. Divide the class into four teams. Pass out one "Weather Bear" to each team, and let them know what type of weather each bear will need to be outfitted for by reading the title on the assigned "Weather Bear." Explain to the students that the goal of the game is to be the first team to earn all three "Weather Items" for their bears.

4. Select any student to spin the spinner on the "Weather Wheel," and state the type of weather indicated by where the paper clip lands. The team that has been assigned that particular type of weather wins that round and may select one of the "Weather Items" for their bear from the pocket chart to place on their "Weather Bear." The game continues in this manner, with a different student selected to spin the wheel each time, until one of the teams earns all three "Weather Items."

5. Pass out the remaining "Weather Items" to the other teams. Have each team color and cut out their items and glue them to their "Weather Bear" cards. Have each team share their bear when everyone is finished.

Adaptations

- Play the same game with small groups of four students. Pass out a "Weather Bear" to each student, and play the game as described above.
- Ask the students to draw a picture of the activities they like to do on rainy, snowy, sunny, or windy days to share with the class.

Related Books

Whatever the Weather by Karen Wallace

Bear Gets Dressed by Harriet Ziefert

Weather Bear Picture Cards

Rainy

Snowy

#50700   *Early Childhood Vocabulary Development Activities*

Sunny

Windy

Weather Wheel

#50700 *Early Childhood Vocabulary Development Activities*

Weather Bear

Weather Items

#50700   *Early Childhood Vocabulary Development Activities*

Weather Items (cont.)

Musical Movements

Skill:

Recognizing movement words

Suggested Group Size:

Whole class

Activity Overview:

Students practice different movements by playing a musical chairs game.

Materials:

- "Movement Cards" (pages 138–139)
- student chairs (one less than the number of students playing)
- music from the radio, a CD, or a cassette tape

Vocabulary Words:

crawling	skipping
flying	swimming
hopping	tip-toeing
running	walking

Activity Preparation

1. Photocopy the "Movement Cards" onto cardstock paper, and color as desired (or print color copies from the CD).
2. Cut out the cards, and laminate for durability.
3. Arrange chairs in two rows. The rows of chairs should be facing back-to-back.

Building Background

Explain to the students that people and animals can move in many ways to get from one place to another. Ask the students to brainstorm how they might move from one side of the classroom to the other. List their responses on the board. Tell the students that today they will be learning some movement words by playing a game called "Musical Movements."

Activity Procedure

1. Have the students stand in a circle around the chairs. Show the students the "Movement Cards," one at a time. Model how to do each movement, and then have the students practice performing each movement as they walk clockwise around the rows of chairs.

2. Tell the students that they will be playing a game similar to "Musical Chairs." Have a student select one of the movement cards and show it to the class. Explain to the students that when the music begins, they should perform that movement as they move around the chairs. When the music stops, each student tries to find a seat. Since there is one fewer chair than there are students, one student will not have a seat. This student will get to select the next movement card, and the game continues in this manner. The game ends when the final "Movement Card" has been played.

Adaptations

- Select a student to perform one of the movements in front of the class. Have the other students guess which movement the student is performing.

- Photocopy the "Animal Sort Cards" (pages 140–141) onto cardstock paper, and color as desired (or make color copies from the CD). Cut out the cards, and laminate for durability. Have the students sort the "Animal Sort Cards" by the way each animal moves.

Related Books

The Hokey Pokey by Larry La Prise

Swing, Slither, or Swim: A Book about Animal Movements by Patricia Stockland

Animal Action ABC by Karen Pandell

crawling

flying

hopping

running

skipping

swimming

tip-toeing

walking

Animal Sort Cards

#50700   *Early Childhood Vocabulary Development Activities*

Animal Sort Cards *(cont.)*

Odd Man Out

Skill:

Recognizing body parts

Suggested Group Size:

Whole class (An odd number of students is needed.)

Activity Overview:

Students will find a partner to connect with to avoid being the "Odd Man Out."

Materials:

- "Body Parts Cards" (pages 144–147)
- 13 bandages

Vocabulary Words:

ankle
back
elbow
forehead
knee
shoulder
stomach
wrist

Activity Preparation

1. Photocopy "Body Parts Cards" onto cardstock, and color as desired (or print color copies from the CD).
2. Cut out the cards, and laminate for durability.
3. Make an outline of a person by having a child lie on a piece of butcher paper and then tracing around him or her.
4. Find an area outside to play in. A basketball court is an ideal size. If a basketball court is unavailable, use jump ropes or cones to designate the area in which the students may play.

Building Background

Have the students dance the "Hokey Pokey" together. Explain to the students that they will be playing a game called "Odd Man Out" that refers to parts of the body. However, the parts of the body they will use in this game may be different from the ones in "Hokey Pokey."

Activity Procedure

1. Show the students the body outline. Have a volunteer select one of the "Body Parts Cards," and have him or her find that part on the body outline. Have the volunteer place a bandage on that body part. Write the name of the body part next to the bandage. Continue in this manner until all of the "Body Parts Cards" have been introduced to the students.

2. Take the students outside to the designated play area to play "Odd Man Out." Select a volunteer to be the odd man out for the first round. The volunteer selects a "Body Parts Card" and hands it to you. If the ankle card was selected, for example, shout out "Ankles!" to the class. Each student, including the odd man out, would quickly find a partner, and stand ankle-to-ankle with him or her. Because there is an odd number of students, there will always be an odd man out. Have the new odd man out come to you to select the next "Body Parts Card" as the partners walk around the area, ankle-to-ankle, until you blow the whistle, and announce the next body part. The game continues in this manner until all "Body Parts Cards" have been played.

Adaptations

- Photocopy enough of the "Paper Doll Boy" (page 148) and the "Paper Doll Girl" (page 149) for each student to use for further practice with the vocabulary words. Have the students use their crayons to complete the instructions you give to them. For example, you might ask the students to draw a red wristwatch on their doll's wrist or a blue headband on the forehead.

- Give the students who need a challenge the opportunity to label the body parts on their paper dolls with words from the vocabulary list.

Related Books

Good Night, Feet by Constance Morgenstern

Here Are My Hands by Bill Martin Jr. and John Archambault

Body Parts Cards

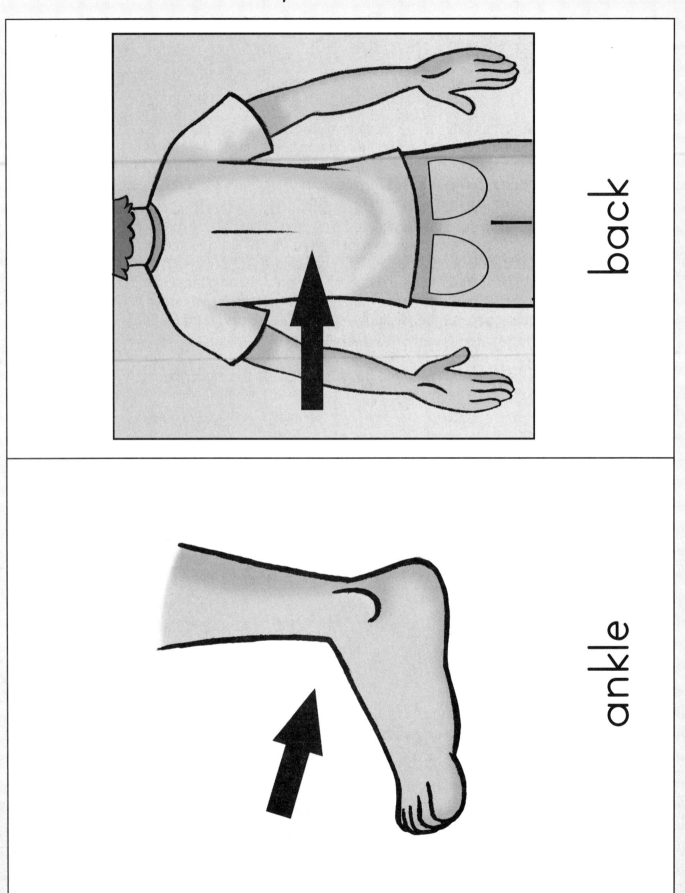

back

ankle

forehead

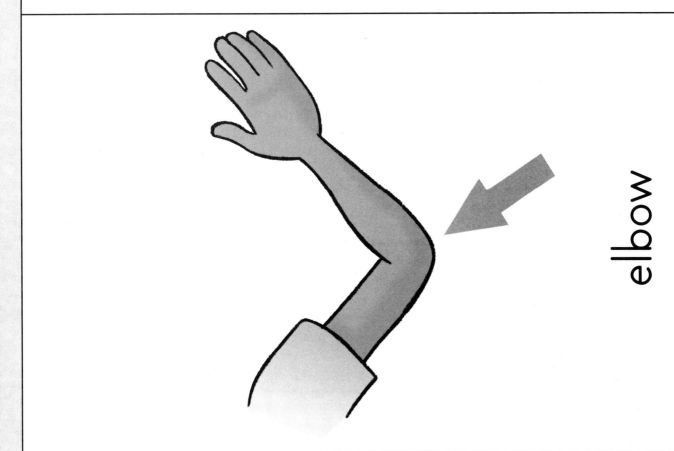

elbow

Body Parts Cards *(cont.)*

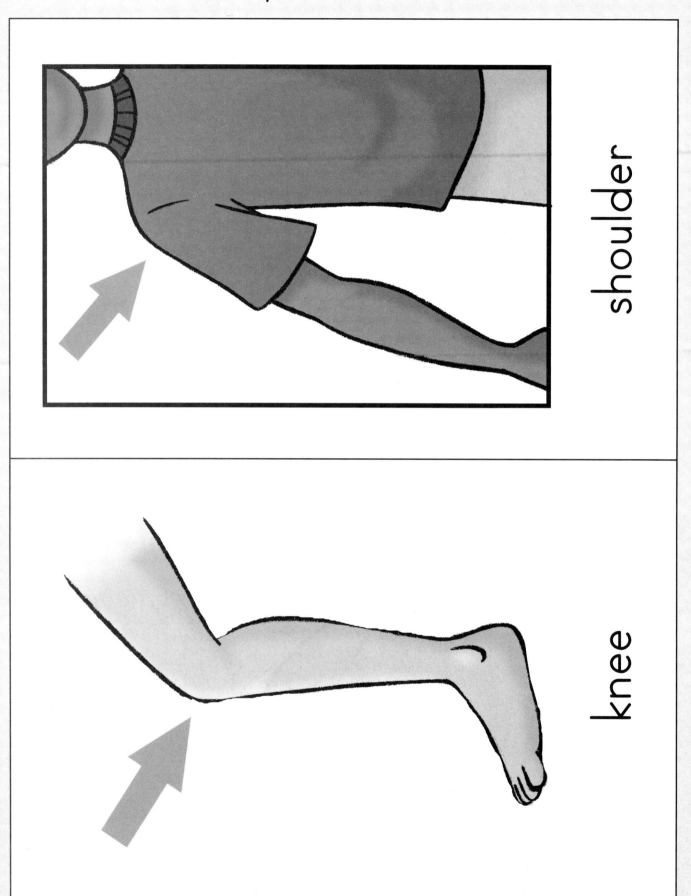

shoulder

knee

#50700   *Early Childhood Vocabulary Development Activities*

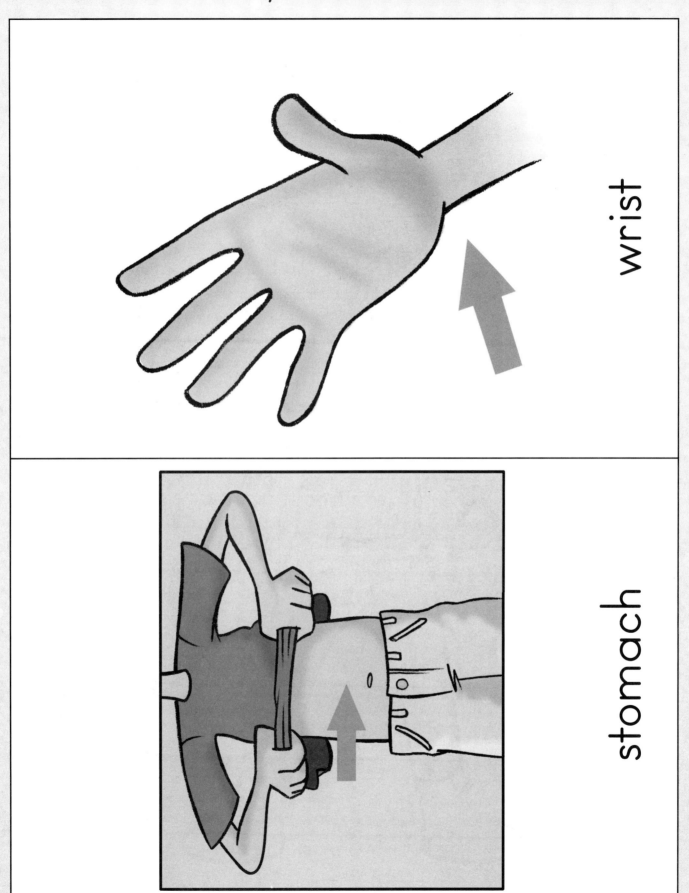

wrist

stomach

Paper Doll Boy

#50700   Early Childhood Vocabulary Development Activities

Paper Doll Girl

Using My Senses: Hearing

Skill:

Recognizing words related to the sense of hearing

Suggested Group Size:

Whole class or small group

Activity Overview:

Students will determine the name of objects hidden from view based on the sound each object makes.

Materials:

- "I Use My Senses Song" (page 160)
- "Ear Picture Card" (page 166)
- variety of noisemakers (whistle, drum, bell, pencil rolling across a desk, etc.)

Vocabulary Words:

ears	loud
hearing	quiet
sound	soft

Activity Preparation

1. Make a poster or transparency of "I Use My Senses Song."
2. Photocopy "Ear Picture Card" onto cardstock paper, and color as desired (or print color copies from the CD).
3. Cut out "Ear Picture Card," and laminate it for durability.
4. Place noisemakers in a bag or box so the students will not be able to see them.

Building Background

Take the students on a listening walk outside, and ask them to remember as many sounds as they can. When you have returned, ask the students to share the kinds of loud sounds that they heard. Explain that loud sounds are sounds that you can hear even if you are far away from the objects that made them. Make a list of their responses on the board. Then ask the students to share the kinds of soft or quiet sounds that they heard. Explain that soft or quiet sounds are sounds you can hear only if you are close to the objects that make them. Make a list of those responses as well. Tell the students that today they will be learning about one of our five senses: our sense of hearing. Show the students the "Ear Picture Card," and read the sentence on the card to them.

Activity Procedure

1. Teach the students the portion of the "I Use My Senses Song" that pertains to hearing.

2. Tell the students that they will be playing a sound guessing game, and they will need to use their sense of hearing to guess what objects are making the sounds that they will hear. Show the students the bag or box of objects, and let them know that there are some mystery noisemakers inside. Select a volunteer to sit in a chair in front of the class. Stand behind the student, and take out one of the noisemakers. Ask the student to listen to the sound your mystery object makes. After using the object to make a sound, have the student guess what the object is. If the child has difficulty, give him or her a hint.

3. After the student correctly guesses the name of the object, have the class vote on whether they think the object made a soft sound or a loud sound. Add the object to the list you already started. Then have the class sing the "I Use My Ears to Hear" song as the student selects the next volunteer to sit in the chair. Continue with the same procedure until you have used all of the noisemakers.

Adaptations

- Discuss onomatopoeia, which are words that sound like the noises they describe, with the students. Show the students samples of children's books or cartoons that use onomatopoeic words.

- Read *Loud and Quiet: An Animal Opposites Book* by Lisa Bullard to the students. The book gives wonderful examples of the difference between loud sounds and quiet sounds.

Related Books

My Five Senses by Aliki

Hearing by Rebecca Olien

Using My Senses: Smelling

Skill:

Recognizing words related to the sense of smell

Suggested Group Size:

Whole class or small group

Activity Overview:

Students will use their sense of smell to name mystery smells.

Materials:

- "I Use My Senses Song" (page 160)
- "Nose Word Cards" (page 165)
- "Baggie Tags" (page 161)
- zipper baggies, one for each student, plus one for you
- "Nose Picture Card" (page 166)
- scented object from home

Vocabulary Words:

nose
smell
scent

Activity Preparation

1. Make a poster or transparency of "I Use My Senses Song"
2. Photocopy enough of "Baggie Tags" so that there is one for each student (or print copies from the CD).
3. Cut out the tags. Staple one tag to each baggie, making sure that the baggie can still be zipped closed.
4. Place a scented object in one of the baggies.
5. Photocopy "Nose Picture Card" and "Nose Word Cards" onto cardstock paper, and color as desired (or print color copies from the CD).
6. Cut out the "Nose Picture Card" and "Nose Word Cards," and laminate for durability.

Building Background

Show the students the object in your baggie that you brought from home. Tell the students that you brought in this object because it has a scent or a smell that you like. Show them the "Nose Word Cards." Tell the students that today they will be learning about one of our five senses—our sense of smell. Show the students the "Nose Picture Card," and read the sentence on the card to them.

Activity Procedure

1. Teach the students the portion of the "I Use My Senses Song" that pertains to smelling.

2. Ask the students to brainstorm the things that have scents or smells that they like. Let the students know that their parents or guardians will have homework tonight. Pass out a baggie to each student. Read aloud the rhyme on the tag. Tell the students that tonight one of their parents or guardians will need to help them select objects to bring to school in the baggie tomorrow. The object that each student selects should have a scent that he or she likes.

3. When the students return their baggies, allow time for them to share what they brought.

Adaptations

- Collect scented stickers. Place each sticker on an index card. Have the students take turns smelling the stickers without looking at them and guess the name of each object that has that scent.

- Have the students sort the scented sticker cards into two groups: scents they like and scents they dislike.

Related Books

My Five Senses by Aliki

Smelling by Rebecca Olien

Using My Senses: Touching

Skill:

Recognizing words related to the sense of touch

Suggested Group Size:

Small groups (4–6 students)

Activity Overview:

Students will feel objects and select the correct texture word to describe how the objects feel.

Materials:

- "Hands Picture Card" (page 167)
- "I Use My Senses Song" (page 160)
- "Texture Word Cards" (page 162)
- 1" (2.5 cm) length or square of the following textured items: sandpaper, scouring pad, tinfoil, wrapping paper, cotton ball, feather, bubble gum, masking tape
- eight 3" (8 cm) squares of construction paper
- poster board or transparency
- pocket chart

Vocabulary Words:

texture	rough
touch	sticky
feel	soft
smooth	

Activity Preparation

1. Make a poster or transparency of "I Use My Senses Song."
2. Photocopy "Texture Word Cards" onto cardstock paper, and color as desired (or print color copies from the CD).
3. Cut out the cards, and laminate for durability.
4. Glue one set of each textured item to a square piece of construction paper.

Building Background

Ask the students to vote on whether they would prefer to sleep on a bed made of sandpaper, chewing gum, or cotton balls. Have the students share their reasons for their selections. Discuss how each item has a different feel or texture to it. Tell the students that today they will be learning about one of our five senses—our sense of touch. Show the students the "Hands Picture Card," and read the sentence on the card to them.

Activity Procedure

1. Teach the students the portion of the "I Use My Senses Song" that pertains to touching.

2. Show the students the "Texture Word Card" that has the title *Texture,* and place it in the pocket chart. Explain to the students that texture is how something feels when you touch it. Then place the other four "Texture Word Cards" in a row on the pocket chart below the Texture card. Tell the students that each card is a texture word or a word that tells how something feels.

3. Place the eight textured items on the table in random order. Point to the "Texture Word Card" that says smooth, and tell the students that there are two items on the table that are smooth. Give them some ideas of other common items that are smooth to which they can all relate. Ask for volunteers to find the two smooth items on the table, and have the students place them in the pocket chart under the "Texture Word Card" that says *smooth.*

4. Repeat this process with the remaining items.

Adaptations

- Make more texture word cards using vocabulary words not on this list, such as wet, bumpy, slippery, or furry. Find some sample texture items to match the new vocabulary words.

- Make a texture word poster to which students may refer. Glue textured items or pictures next to each word on the list.

Related Books

My Five Senses by Aliki

Touching by Rebecca Olien

Is It Rough? Is It Smooth? Is It Shiny? by Tana Hoban

Using My Senses:
Tasting

Skill:
Using appropriate vocabulary to describe how things taste

Suggested Group Size:

Small group (3–6 students)

Activity Overview:

Students will taste items and describe them as being salty, sweet, sour, or bitter.

Materials:

- "Tongue Picture Card" (page 167)
- "I Use My Senses Song" (page 160)
- "Taste Word Cards" (page 163)
- items for tasting: sugar, salt, unsweetened chocolate or baking soda, lemon juice
- various types of baby food in jars
- craft sticks or coffee stirrers
- 4 small containers (empty baby food jars or paper cups)

Vocabulary Words:

taste	salty
tongue	bitter
sweet	sour

Activity Preparation

1. Photocopy "Tongue Picture Card" onto cardstock paper, and color as desired (or print color copies from the CD).
2. Laminate "Tongue Picture Card" for durability.
3. Make a poster or transparency of "I Use My Senses Song."
4. Fill one container halfway with sugar, and label it "Sweet," using a permanent marker. Fill a second container halfway with salt, and label it "Salty." Fill a third container halfway with unsweetened chocolate or baking soda, and label it "Bitter." Fill a fourth container halfway with lemon juice, and label it "Sour."
5. Remove the labels from the jars of baby food. Place each label upside down under its jar.
6. Be aware of any food allergies your students might have or foods that they are not allowed to eat before beginning the activity.

Building Background

Ask the students if they know what it means if someone says, "She has a sweet tooth." Discuss how some people enjoy foods that taste sweet. Then have the students brainstorm foods that they think are sweet. Tell the students that today they will be learning about one of our five senses—our sense of taste. Show the students the four "Taste Word Cards," and explain that our tongues not only sense sweet foods, but salty, bitter, and sour foods as well. Show the students the "Tongue Picture Card," and read the sentence on the card to them.

Activity Procedure

1. Gather the students around a table and show them the four labeled containers. These will be used as a reference for the students throughout the activity. Before beginning, be sure to let the students know that they should never taste unknown foods without permission from an adult that they know and trust. Also, the students will be using the craft sticks or coffee stirrers as spoons to taste the different items. Therefore, it is important to model how to use the "spoons" properly and how to discard them after each taste so as not to transfer germs to others.

2. Pass out a "spoon" to the students and have them take turns dipping them into a container, tasting the item, and then throwing away the "spoons." Be sure that they have a good foundation for understanding the differences among sweet, salty, bitter, and sour tastes.

3. Teach the students the portion of the "I Use My Senses Song" that pertains to tasting.

4. Show the students the first baby food jar. Tell the students that they need to be "taste detectives" and use their sense of taste to decide whether the baby food is sweet, salty, bitter, or sour. Have the students use "spoons" to taste the baby food. Then have the group vote on which of those four basic tastes they think the baby food has. If a student has difficulty deciding, have him or her refer to the four labeled containers for support. Show the students the baby food label and discuss which basic taste it has. Repeat the procedure with the remaining jars of baby food.

Adaptations

- Let the students know that there is actually a fifth basic taste that has been identified, called *umami.* This basic taste is said to be synonymous with "meaty" or "savory" and has only recently been added to the list of basic tastes.

- Instead of using baby food, use various flavored jelly beans.

Related Books

My Five Senses by Aliki

Tasting by Rebecca Olien

Using My Senses: Seeing

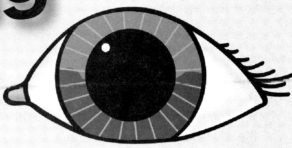

Skill:

Understanding vocabulary related to the sense of sight

Suggested Group Size:

Whole class or small group

Activity Overview:

Students will draw two pictures and compare the one in which they were able to use their sense of sight to the one in which they were not able to use their sense of sight.

Materials:

- "Eyes Picture Card" (page 168)
- "I Use My Senses Song" (page 160)
- "Seeing Word Cards" (page 164)
- blank paper and crayons for each student

Vocabulary Words:

seeing	size
eyes	shape
color	

Activity Preparation

1. Photocopy "Eyes Picture Card" and "Seeing Word Cards" onto cardstock paper, and color as desired (or print color copies from the CD).
2. Laminate "Eyes Picture Card" for durability.
3. Cut out the "Seeing Word Cards."
4. Make a poster or transparency of the "I Use My Senses Song."

Building Background

Ask the students if they have ever played a game called *Pin the Tail on the Donkey*. Discuss how the game is played, emphasizing the use of a blindfold as the player tries to pin the tail as close to the end of the donkey as possible. Ask the students what would happen if one of the players did not wear the blindfold. Tell the students that today they will be learning about one of our five senses—our sense of sight. Show the students the "Eyes Picture Card," and read the sentence on the card to them. Let the students know that they will be playing another game in which they will see how their sense of sight will help them.

Activity Procedure

1. Pass out a piece of blank paper to each student. Tell the students that they will have one minute to draw a picture of the American flag. Discuss the colors and the numbers of stripes and stars on the flag. The students will need to place a box of crayons in front of them as well. Time them as they draw their flags. When time is up, have the students share their pictures.

2. Pass out a second piece of blank paper to each student. Tell them that they will be drawing the flag once again, this time without relying on their sense of sight. Have each student place the paper on a book, which will act as a portable table. Make sure each student has a box of crayons in front of him or her. The students will be drawing the picture with the paper and "book table" upon their heads and with their eyes closed. As soon as everyone has their eyes closed, say "Go!" Time them as they draw their flags again. When time is up, have the students compare their two pictures.

3. Show the students the "Seeing Word Cards," and discuss how we rely on our eyes to see the color, the size, and the shape of objects around us. Ask the students to once again compare their two pictures. This time have them compare the size, the shape, and the colors used on their two pictures.

4. Teach the students the portion of the "I Use My Senses Song" that pertains to seeing.

Adaptations

- You may first want to model this activity for the students. Show them how to hold the book and paper while drawing the picture. Share your picture with the students before they attempt to draw theirs.

- Try playing a game of *Pin the Tail on the Donkey* with the students.

Related Books

My Five Senses by Aliki

Seeing by Rebecca Olien

I Use My Senses Song

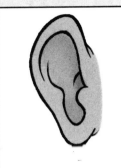

(Sung to the tune of "The Farmer in the Dell")

I use my ears to hear.
I use my ears to hear.
Loud sounds I can hear from far,
And soft sounds when I'm near.

I use my nose to smell.
I use my nose to smell.
Some scents I like, and some I don't
By sniffing I can tell.

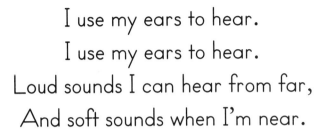
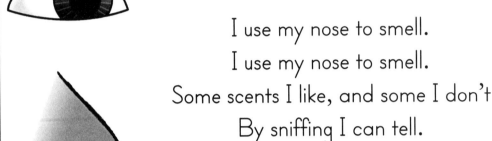

I use my hands to touch.
I use my hands to touch,
To feel some textures smooth and soft
And some so very rough.

I use my tongue to taste.
I use my tongue to taste,
Salty, sour, bitter, sweet,
Each one has its place.

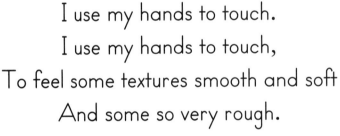
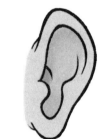
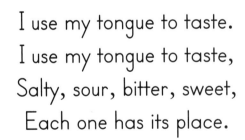

I use my eyes to see.
I use my eyes to see,
The color, size, and shape of things,
That are around me.

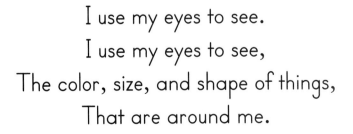

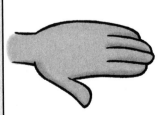

Baggie Tags

Please help me take a look and see
If there's an object just for me,
One that has my favorite smell
To take to school for Show and Tell.
Just place the object in this bag
And write my name upon this tag.

Name _____

Please help me take a look and see
If there's an object just for me,
One that has my favorite smell
To take to school for Show and Tell.
Just place the object in this bag
And write my name upon this tag.

Name _____

Please help me take a look and see
If there's an object just for me,
One that has my favorite smell
To take to school for Show and Tell.
Just place the object in this bag
And write my name upon this tag.
Name _____

Please help me take a look and see
If there's an object just for me,
One that has my favorite smell
To take to school for Show and Tell.
Just place the object in this bag
And write my name upon this tag.
Name _____

Please help me take a look and see
If there's an object just for me,
One that has my favorite smell
To take to school for Show and Tell.
Just place the object in this bag
And write my name upon this tag.

Name _____

Please help me take a look and see
If there's an object just for me,
One that has my favorite smell
To take to school for Show and Tell.
Just place the object in this bag
And write my name upon this tag.

Name _____

Please help me take a look and see
If there's an object just for me,
One that has my favorite smell
To take to school for Show and Tell.
Just place the object in this bag
And write my name upon this tag.
Name _____

Please help me take a look and see
If there's an object just for me,
One that has my favorite smell
To take to school for Show and Tell.
Just place the object in this bag
And write my name upon this tag.
Name _____

Texture

smooth

rough

sticky

soft

#50700 *Early Childhood Vocabulary Development Activities*

Taste Word Cards

sweet

salty

bitter

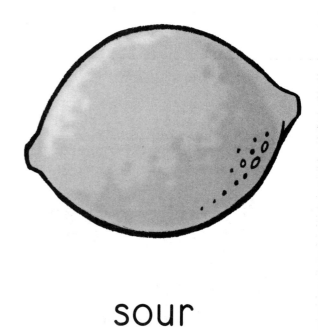

sour

Seeing Word Cards

color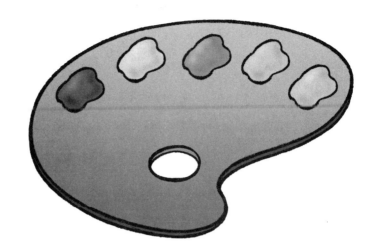

size

shape

#50700   *Early Childhood Vocabulary Development Activities*

Nose Word Cards

nose

smell

scent

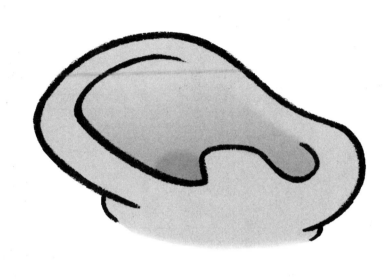

I use my ears to hear.

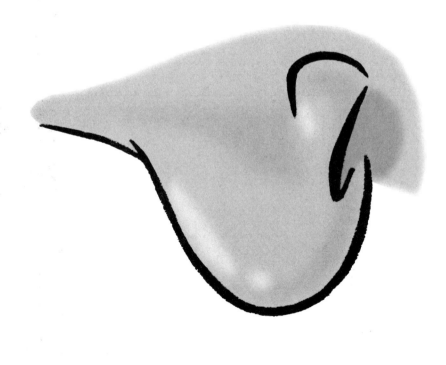

I use my nose to smell.

Hand Picture Card and Tongue Picture Card

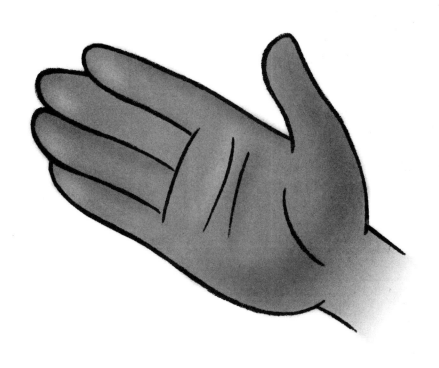

I use my hands to feel or touch.

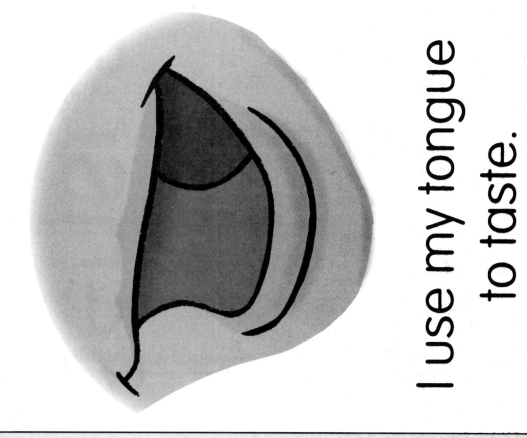

I use my tongue to taste.

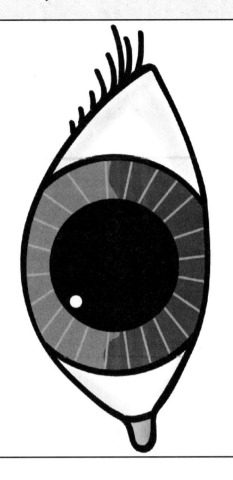

I use my eyes
to see.

The
5
Senses

Appendix A

References Cited

Anderson, R., and W. Nagy. 1993. The vocabulary conundrum, Technical report no. 570. Urbana, Illinois: Center for the Study of Reading.

Baker, S., D. Simmons, and E. Kame'enui. 1995. Vocabulary acquisition: Curricular and instructional implications for diverse learners, Technical report no. 14. Prepared by the National Center to Improve the Tools of Educators, funded by the U.S. Office of Special Education Programs.

Beck, I., M. McKeown, and L. Kucan. 2002. *Bringing words to life: Robust vocabulary instruction.* New York: Guilford Press.

Blachowicz, C., P. Fisher, and S. Watts-Taffe. 2005. Integrated vocabulary instruction: Meeting the needs of diverse learners in grades K-5. Naperville, Illinois: Learning Point Associates, sponsored under government contract number ED-01-CO-0011.

Center for the Improvement of Early Reading Achievement (CIERA). 2001. Put reading first: The research building blocks for teaching children to read. Funded by the National Institute for Literacy (NIFL).

DeGross, M. 1994. *Donovan's word jar.* New York: HarperCollins Children's Books.

Graves, M., and S. Watts-Taffe. 2002. The place of word consciousness in a research-based vocabulary program. In *What research says about reading instruction*, eds. A. E. Farstrup and S. J. Samuels, 140–165. Newark, Delaware: International Reading Association.

Moore, P., and A. Lyon. 2005. *New essentials for teaching reading in pre-K–2.* New York: Scholastic, Inc.

Appendix B: Recommended Books

Albert, Burton. *Where Does the Trail Lead?* New York: Simon & Schuster, 1991.

Aliki. *My Five Senses.* New York: HarperCollins Publishers, 1989.

Anholt, Catherine, and Laurence Anholt. *What Makes Me Happy?* Cambridge, Massachusetts: Candlewick Press, 1994.

Bennette Hopkins, Lee. *School Supplies: A Book of Poems.* New York: Alladin Picture Books, 2000.

Brown, Margaret Wise. *Bumble Bugs and Elephants.* New York: HarperCollins, 2006.

Brown, Margaret Wise. *My World of Color.* New York: Scholastic Inc., 2002.

Bryant, Megan E. *Shape Spotters.* New York: Grosset & Dunlap, 2002.

Bullard, Lisa. *Loud and Quiet: An Animal Opposites Book.* Mankato, Minnesota: Capstone Press, 2006.

Calmenson, Stephanie. *Zip, Whiz, Zoom!* Boston: Little Brown and Company, 1992.

Carrick, Carol. *Patrick's Dinosaurs.* New York: Clarion Books, 1983.

Cleary, Brian. *How Much Can a Bare Bear Bear?* Minneapolis, Minnesota: Millbrook Press, 2005.

DeGross, Monalisa. *Donovan's Word Jar.* New York: HarperCollins Children's Books, 1994.

DeRolf, Shane. *The Crayon Box That Talked.* New York: Random House, Inc., 1997.

Donaldson, Julia. *The Spiffiest Giant in Town.* New York: Dial Books for Young Readers, 2002.

Eastman, P.D. *Big Dog, Little Dog.* New York: Beginner Books, 2003.

Edwards, Wallace. *Monkey Business.* New York: Kids Can Press Ltd., 2004.

Ehlert, Lois. *Color Farm.* Printed in China: Harper Festival, A Division of HarperCollins Publishers, 1990.

Firestone, Mary. *Community Helpers: School Secretaries.* Mankato, Minnesota: Capstone Press, 2003.

Gwynne, Fred. *A Chocolate Moose for Dinner.* New York: Simon and Schuster Books for Young Readers, 1980.

Gwynne, Fred. *The King Who Rained.* New York: Windmill/Wander Books, 1980.

Hendra, Sue. *Flip and Find: Opposites.* Cambridge, Massachusetts: Candlewick Press, 1999.

Hoban, Tana. *All About Where.* New York: Greenwillow Books, 1991.

Hoban, Tana. *Is It Rough? Is It Smooth? Is It Shiny?* New York: Greenwillow Books, 1984.

Hoberman, Mary Ann. *A House Is a House for Me.* New York: Viking Press, 1978.

Johnson, Paul. *On Top of Spaghetti.* New York: Scholastic Press, 2006.

Kirk, Daniel. *GO!* New York: Hyperion Books for Children, 2001.

Kittinger, Jo. *Moving Day.* New York: Children's Press, 2003.

La Prise, Larry. *The Hokey Pokey.* New York: Simon and Schuster Books for Young Children, 1996.

Maestro, Betsy, and Giulio Maestro. *All Aboard Overnight: A Book of Compound Words.* New York: Clarion Books, 1992.

Martin Jr., Bill, John Archambault, and Ted Rand. *Here Are My Hands.* New York: Holt, 1987.

Marzollo, Jean. *I Spy School Days.* New York: Scholastic: 2005.

Mayo, Margaret. *Choo Choo Clickety-Clack!* Minneapolis, Minnesota: Carolrhoda Books, 2004.

Appendix B: Recommended Books *(cont.)*

McGrory, Anik. *Kidogo*. New York: Bloomsburg Children's Books, distributed by Holtzbrinck Publishers, 2005.

Morgenstern, Constance. *Good Night, Feet*. New York: H. Holt, 1991.

Morris, Ann. *That's Our Nurse!* Brookfield, Connecticut: The Millbrook Press, 2003.

Morris, Ann. *That's Our Principal!* Brookfield, Connecticut: The Millbrook Press, 2003.

Muehlenhardt, Amy. *Drawing and Learning About Dinosaurs: Using Shapes and Lines*. Minneapolis, Minnesota: Picture Window Books, 2004.

Olien, Rebecca. *Hearing*. Mankato, Minnesota: Capstone Press, 2005.

Olien, Rebecca. *Seeing*. Mankato, Minnesota: Capstone Press, 2005.

Olien, Rebecca. *Smelling*. Mankato, Minnesota: Capstone Press, 2005.

Olien, Rebecca. *Tasting*. Mankato, Minnesota: Capstone Press, 2006.

Olien, Rebecca. *Touching*. Mankato, Minnesota: Capstone Press, 2006.

Oliver, Dennis. *ESL Idiom Page*, **http://www.eslcafe.com/idioms/** (accessed April 10, 2007).

Pandell, Karen. *Animal Action ABC*. New York: Dutton Children's Books, 1996.

Pinkney, Sandra L. *A Rainbow All Around Me*. New York: Scholastic Inc., 2002.

Potter, Keith. *This and That: Doodlezoo: A Book of Opposites*. San Francisco: Chronicle Books, 1999.

Pluckrose, Henry. *Eating and Tasting*. Austin, Texas: Raintree Steck-Vaughn, 1998.

Rosen, Michael. *We're Going on a Bear Hunt*. New York: Margaret K. McElderry Books, 1989.

Schertle, Alice. *The Skeleton in the Closet*. Manufactured in China: HarperCollins Publishers, 2003.

Seeger, Laura Vaccaro. *Walter Was Worried*. New Milford, Connecticut: Roaring Books Press, 2005.

Snodgrass, Catherine. *Super Silly Sayings That Are Over Your Head: A Children's Illustrated Book of Idioms*. Higganum, Connecticut: Starfish Specialty Press, 2004.

Stockland, Patricia. *Swing, Slither, or Swim: A Book About Animal Movements*. Minneapolis, Minnesota: Picture Window Books, 2005.

Terban, Marvin. *Eight Ate: A Feast of Homonym Riddles*. New York: Clarion Books, 1982.

Trattles, Patricia. *Flying Butter*. New York: Scholastic Inc., 2005.

Wallace, Karen. *Whatever the Weather*. New York: DK Publishing, 1999.

Walton, Rick. *Once There Was a Bull...(Frog)*. Salt Lake City, Utah: Gibbs Smith Publisher, 1995.

Weber, Rebecca. *How We Travel*. Minneapolis, Minnesota: Compass Point Books, 2005.

Wolff, Ferida. *It Is the Wind*. New York: HarperCollins Publishers, 2005.

Ziefert, Harriet. *Bear Gets Dressed*. New York: Sterling Publishing Co., Inc. 2004.

Appendix C: Picture Dictionary Template

#50700 *Early Childhood Vocabulary Development Activities*

My Picture Dictionary

By _____

Appendix C: Quarter It Template

My Definition

My Sentence

My Word

My Picture

#50700   *Early Childhood Vocabulary Development Activities*

Appendix D: Book Page

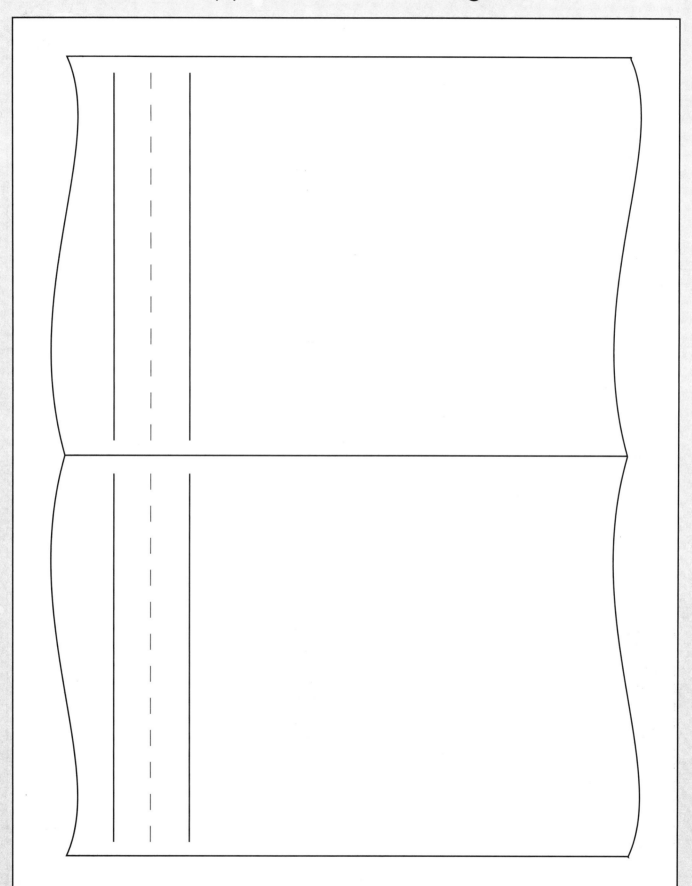

Appendix E: Blank Flip Cards